CHILDREN
of the
PROMISE

CHILDREN
of the
PROMISE

The Biblical Case for Infant Baptism

ROBERT R. BOOTH

PUBLISHING
P.O.BOX 817 • PHILLIPSBURG • NEW JERSEY 08865-0817

Unless otherwise indicated, Scripture quotations are from the New American Standard Bible. Copyright by the Lockman Foundation 1960, 1962, 1963, 1968, 1971, 1973, 1975, 1977.

Printed in the United States of America

Library of Congress Cataloging-in-Publication Data

Booth, Robert R., 1955–
 Children of the promise : the Biblical case for infant baptism / Robert R. Booth.
   p. cm.
 Includes bibliographical references and index.
 ISBN 0-87552-165-7 (pbk.)
 1. Infant baptism. 2. Infant baptism—Biblical teaching.
3. Covenants—Religious aspects—Reformed Church. 4. Reformed Church—Doctrines. 5. Covenants—Religious aspects—Presbyterian Church. 6. Presbyterian Church—Doctrines. I. Title.
BV813.B66 1995
234'.1612—dc20   95-25487

To my children
and my children's children

Contents

Foreword

IT IS ALWAYS EXCITING to learn of the publication of another book having to do with infant baptism. Far too frequently, those who oppose the practice think that there is no biblical basis for it and that it is little more than an unfortunate holdover from Roman Catholicism. They sometimes misrepresent the practice as a means of forgiving sins. That, of course, is not true. The truth about infant baptism is clearly set forth in *Children of the Promise*. And, best of all, the argument of the book is based solely upon biblical exposition; there is no other way in which true paedobaptists wish to debate the question.

Presbyterians and others who hold to the biblical practice of infant baptism will welcome this book. Indeed, it is my hope that many Baptists will do so as well. Robert Booth, the author, is himself a former Baptist who, by studying the Scriptures, came to see the importance of the covenant of grace in understanding the issues involved. Because of his gentle and sympathetic approach, I think many Baptists will appreciate his teaching–even if in the end they cannot yet agree with him.

He knows the Baptist way of thinking and deals with it kindly, but firmly.

The illustrative materials with which he introduces many of his chapters also greatly facilitate the understanding of the points made in those chapters. Here, in one volume, you will find much cogent information (some old, some new) presented in a clear, helpful manner. I think it will make an impact on Christ's church. I heartily commend it to you.

JAY E. ADAMS
ENOREE, SOUTH CAROLINA

Preface

We may compromise with conscience for half the price,
but God will not endorse the compromise, and like Ananias and
Sapphira, we will lose not only what we thought we had purchased
so cheaply, but also the price we paid for it.[1]—T. V. Moore

CONTROVERSY IS EASIER LEFT ALONE. Perhaps our lives would be less difficult if we followed the elementary school instructions of "be quiet, get in line, and don't bother your neighbor." None of us likes the disruption of change. Nevertheless, God calls us to live lives of change—sometimes excruciatingly painful change. Various sources challenge us to rethink our positions, to go to the Scriptures over and over, and to adjust our thinking and lives accordingly—this is the process of sanctification.

For a number of years, I avoided dealing with the controversial subject of baptism. I had close friends on both sides of this controversy—Baptists and paedobaptists (believers in infant baptism)—and therefore I was acutely aware of the passions on both sides of this debate. For ten years as a Baptist pastor, my desire to study this thorny issue seriously was easily pushed aside to be dealt with at a later and more convenient time. I think we often avoid studying a matter because we fear that our views will not be confirmed. God allowed me to wait no longer. In his kind providence, it pleased him to bring this matter to bear upon me, and so the dreaded journey began.

As I began studying the subject of baptism and realized that my views were being challenged, I felt my heart sink. Day by day I could sense myself moving further and further in the direction I did not want to go. Finally, there I stood, teetering on the precipice, looking for someone to rescue me. As time pushed forward, I found myself in a real dilemma. As one of the elders at a Baptist church—a church family I had been a part of for fifteen years, a family I loved very much—the last thing I wanted to do was to disrupt the unity of our congregation. But I also knew that the congregation expected me to study the Scriptures and faithfully follow what I believed them to teach. I concluded that my primary obligations were to be faithful to God's Word and to maintain a clear conscience before him. My brothers and sisters in Christ, even if they did not understand or agree with my doctrinal position, would certainly appreciate this commitment to Scripture.

Since my change would potentially affect the lives of so many other people, I determined to write down *my reasons for changing my views*. These reasons may or may not persuade others, but they did persuade me. A written explanation was the least I owed to my fellow church members—an answer to the inevitable question, Why? No other opportunities were available for me to express my convictions to those friends I hold so dear, and so I chose to offer this brief book to any who may wish to read a presentation of the case for baptizing the children of believing parents.

This book has never had as its purpose the fanning of any flames of strife. Moreover, my prayer is that it will promote greater understanding and ultimately contribute to unity in the truth. Christians are often charged with not being able to agree with one another, yet even our disagreements can serve to sharpen us and advance God's kingdom. Richard Baxter's statement seems appropriate.

> The servants of God do mind the matter of religion more seriously than others do; and therefore their differences are made observable to the world. They cannot make light of the smallest truth of God; and this may be some occasion of their indifference; whereas the ungodly differ not about religion, because they have heartily no religion to differ about. Is this a unity and peace to be desired? I had rather have the discord of the saints than such a concord of the wicked.[2]

Finally, my fellow Christians, I must ask you, if the doctrine of infant baptism were true, would you want to know it? Please do not read past this important question or take it lightly. *If the doctrine of infant baptism were true, would you want to know it?* If the answer is no, then I hope you will contemplate the grave implications of such an answer. A positive answer to this question demands from you the serious investigation of this topic and a willingness to be open to God's truth, wherever it may lead, whatever it may cost. You must not deny yourself access to any information that may shed light upon the truth. Those who sincerely and diligently seek the truth will find it; they have no reason to fear being challenged by any contrary view.

Study this doctrine until you understand the various positions. Ask the hard questions of both sides. Ask them again. Enlist the Holy Spirit to guide you as you pray for understanding. Weigh the evidence. Follow the Scriptures alone. God will bless you richly!

Notes

1. T. V. Moore, *Zechariah, Haggai and Malachi,* Geneva Series of Commentaries (1856; reprint, Carlisle, Pa.: Banner of Truth, 1974), 162.

2. I. D. E. Thomas, ed., *The Golden Treasury of Puritan Quotations* (Chicago: Moody Press, 1975), 62.

Acknowledgments

I WOULD LIKE TO THANK my many Christian friends, both in and outside my own congregation, who have prayed for me and provided encouragement through my doctrinal struggles—whether they have agreed or disagreed with my position.

Special thanks and appreciation go to Ben House and Sean Mahaffey for their friendship, prayers, and advice. To Dr. Greg Bahnsen, thank you for your friendship and counsel, and for never pressuring me to do anything other than study God's Word and remain faithful to it. Also, to Doug Wilson, thanks for the encouragement and insights, and for making me laugh when I needed a lift.

Likewise, thanks go to my brothers and sisters in Christ who are wrestling with this issue of baptism and have shown a sincere desire to know the truth of Scripture even when it hurts. I will always be grateful to you for your sincerity, encouragement, and unconditional love, regardless of the position you finally arrive at. To my friends who have graciously opposed my views and sought to persuade me back, I love you and appreciate the sincere love you have for me, for God, and for his Word. I have learned much from you and owe you a great debt of love.

Finally, my deepest thanks and appreciation go to my covenant companion—my wife of twenty-one years and my friend forever, Marinell. Your prayers, understanding, and words of encouragement have made all the difference.

CHAPTER 1

Foundations: Preparing Our Hearts and Minds

AFTER MORNING WORSHIP at Berean Baptist Church one Sunday, Jane and Steve are talking at the back of the sanctuary.

STEVE: Jane, have you heard that Randy [an elder] and a few other members of our church now believe in infant baptism?

JANE: Yeah, I find that hard to imagine.

STEVE: Me too. I wouldn't dream of having our little Rachel baptized—at least not until she's old enough to understand the gospel.

JANE: How could anyone believe in baptizing babies?

STEVE: I have no idea.

RANDY: Excuse me, but I couldn't help hearing you ask how anyone could believe in infant baptism. Were you just expressing shock, or would you really want to know more about that view?

STEVE (a bit startled): Well, I have to admit, we were surprised to hear that you've become a paedobaptist. It seems so foreign to Scripture. But maybe we could sit down and look at what the Bible has to say about it.

RANDY: I'd love to do that. We both believe that the Bible is the only rule of faith and life. Baptism is one of those areas, so let's look and see what the Bible says. I've written down my thoughts on the subject—the things that persuaded me. Would you like to see my reasons for thinking that the Bible supports including our children in God's gracious covenant?

Steve and Jane agree to read Randy's study of the subject and then schedule a time when they can all get together to discuss it.

THIS BOOK FOCUSES on one basic question about baptism: *Who should be baptized?* Baptists maintain that baptism is for believers *only.* Others say that baptism is for believers *and* for their children. Holding to the latter view are Reformed paedobaptists.[1]

Few on either side of this question are well prepared to defend their views from the Bible. This highly emotional issue often produces much heat, but precious little light—many strong assertions, but few biblical arguments. A calmer and more biblical approach to studying and discussing this issue is needed.

Few subjects have divided Christians more than the sacraments: What is a sacrament?[2] What is the nature of a sacrament? How many sacraments are there? Who should receive the sacraments? How are the sacraments to be administered? Who is to administer them? What are the effects of the sacraments? These and many other questions are debated. The intensity of this struggle reflects the importance of these doctrines.

At the foundation of our beliefs are presuppositions, which all of us have, though we may not be aware of them. Francis Schaeffer explained, "Most people catch their presuppositions from their family and surrounding society the way a child catches the measles."[3] Our views of baptism have typically been caught the same way. Perhaps they have come through our parents, or we have picked them up from the church or culture in which we were raised. With these powerful social influences at work, our expectations have been formed. And since we often find what we look for, the Bible is thought to confirm what we have always believed.

The Need for Diligent Study

No one is free from doctrinal error. Our errors demonstrate a failure to love the Lord our God with all our mind. We are not diligent enough in searching the Scriptures to know the mind of God. Much theology tends to be done by the "shoot, ready, aim" method. Careless workmen in the Word of Truth fail to handle that Word accurately (2 Tim. 2:15). I suspect that most of us need to work harder in our studies. The Puritan John Brown described part of the problem when he wrote, "There is no pouring christian truth passively into the minds of men. If men will not listen, and reflect, and examine the meaning of statements, the validity of arguments, and the force of motives, the best possible teaching will not make them wiser or better."[4]

People commonly protect their cherished beliefs, not by a solid, reasoned defense from the Bible, but by carelessly misrepresenting opposing views. Doctrinal insecurity may tempt us to resort to illegitimate means of defending our tenuous convictions. Some, for example, argue that Reformed paedobaptists baptize infants because of the influence of the old Roman Catholic sacerdotal[5] practice. But that is the fallacy of guilt by association. While some people may practice infant baptism because of Roman Catholic influence, it is not fair to presume that all paedobaptists do so for the same reasons.

Some of my theological heroes from the past are men like John Calvin, Charles Hodge, B. B. Warfield, J. Gresham Machen, John Murray, and Cornelius Van Til—men well known for their uncompromising commitment to Scripture. It would be a fantastic claim to suggest, as I have heard it said, that these men hold their position on baptism because they have mindlessly followed Rome. Given their commitment to the principle of "Scripture alone," their rigorous scholarship and careful attention to details, their Christian character, and their profound biblical wisdom on so many other important questions, we should not so easily dismiss their view of baptism. Though they of course are fallible, they are models to us of diligence in searching Scripture—not the traditions of men— for an understanding of issues such as baptism.

Only after considerable struggle do we come to a firm position on many doctrines of Scripture—for example, the Sabbath, the Atonement, and eschatology. Christians may become more confused than ever after some initial study of a particular question. However, we need to press on until the issues becomes clear. That involves considering the best questions and arguments of opposing views and not being swayed by every odd or weak argument we hear. Quick answers are not always right answers. Rightly dividing the Word can be demanding work.

Disagreeing as Brothers

God commands us to love him with all our heart, soul, mind, and strength, and to love our neighbor as ourselves. We are even told to love our enemies. Certainly, then, we are to love our Christian brothers with whom we may disagree. One way we love our neighbor is to conduct ourselves in a godly and just way—to be honest with him and about him.

Christians who hold different doctrinal views often fail this test. Personal pride and the desire to be right may override Christian character, and soon brother sins against brother. Too often we resort to anger, name-calling, mudslinging, questioning the sincerity or honesty of our brother, or other personal attacks. When this occurs, regardless of the theological strength of our arguments, we have lost—we have ceased to be Christian at that point.[6] In defending one truth of Scripture, we are not authorized to disregard the others.

Honest Christians, seeking truth, may disagree on a given

point of doctrine. Nevertheless, we must guard against the temptation to bear false witness against our brother by maliciously or recklessly misrepresenting his views. We need to understand exactly what our brother's positions are before we attempt to expose their weaknesses. How can we possibly oppose what we do not understand?

We know we understand an opposing view only when we are able to articulate it and receive the affirmation of our opponent that we have accurately represented his position. Only then can we proceed to argue against it. It does not take a big man to push over a straw man—little men are up to this simple task.[7] Nor is it enough to say that our brother is wrong, or silly, or that his arguments make no sense; we must be prepared to demonstrate such claims. Some argue they do not need to understand opposing views. But they cannot expect to engage people who disagree with them.

A person may genuinely believe he has seen a UFO. It will, however, take more than his assertion to convince me. Subjective belief, even when it is held with passion, must be substantiated by more than one's own assertions. Likewise, some Christians want others to blindly accept their assertions on baptism even though they may not be able to defend their position biblically. But the faithful Christian will demand solid biblical evidence to demonstrate the truth of any doctrinal position.

Clearly, a divisive or contentious spirit is out of place. But a sincere search for biblical knowledge and understanding should not be construed as divisive or contentious. If our first commitment is to the Bible, there is no topic that is off limits in legitimate inquiry. If, however, unity is preferred over the honest search for biblical truth, or harsh assertions replace solid biblical interchange among fellow Christians, we are no longer thinking like Christians. "Because I said so" replaces "Thus saith the Lord." Censorship of any biblical topic within the church is contrary to the Berean spirit (Acts 17:11) and offers an even greater threat to church unity than the topic at hand.

Censorship cuts off access to legitimate information and

makes any final determinations uncertain and probably un-just. Proverbs 18:17 instructs us, "The first to plead his case seems just, until another comes and examines him." Neither tradition nor power makes a particular position true. Refusal to be cross-examined by our brothers in Christ betrays a not-so-subtle insecurity and a willingness to settle disputes on grounds other than the weight of the biblical evidence. John Calvin warned against the refusal to hear contrary ideas: "The less the interchange of opinion, the greater will be the danger of pernicious dogmatism."[8]

Humility must guide our discussion. This does not forbid expressions of enthusiasm or confidence in one's position; nor does it exclude vigorous exchanges between sincere Christians. It does, however, exclude arrogance, rudeness, and anger. The fruit of the Spirit must be manifest even in our disagreements with one another. Gentleness and reverence argue a cause far more effectively than does invective (1 Peter 3:15). Our goal must be to build up Christ's church, not to divide it. Brothers have often wounded one another needlessly over the topic of baptism with hasty and unkind words. No one has ever won anything in such an exchange—only losers emerge from the fray. Destructive debate is sad, regardless of the topic. It is especially inappropriate in dealing with baptism—a sign of our union with Christ and consequently with one another.

The Challenge

I challenge you to reconsider the issue of who should be bap-tized. It is not an easy thing to do honestly. I know, because this book is the result of such a reconsideration. As a Baptist minister, I had many reasons for avoiding an open examina-tion of this doctrine of baptism. Initially, I set out to find am-munition to use against the paedobaptist position. I found myself wrestling with the temptation to make Scripture conform to my preconceived ideas. My attitude was *I don't want to be a paedobaptist!* But in the end it did not matter what I wanted. It only mattered what the Scriptures taught.

In considering this issue, you too must go to the Word of God, asking the Holy Spirit to lead you into all truth. Examine the Scriptures to see if these things are so. Scripture alone is the referee. For the genuine student of God's Word, a workman who needs not to be ashamed, this challenge to honestly study the issue of baptism will be taken seriously. It is the only right way to resolve the question.

Common Ground

As Bible-believing Christians, Reformed paedobaptists and Baptists have many things in common. Many of us share a common heritage in our confessions of faith. The 1689 London Baptist Confession was deliberately modeled after the Westminster Confession of Faith (1646) in an effort to show Christian unity.[9] This unity of belief should be kept in mind as we explore our differences over baptism. Instead of drawing lines in the dirt and refusing to talk, those of us who love Jesus Christ and his Word must pray, study, listen, think, question, answer, and pray some more.

Besides other things that we agree on as brothers in Christ, we agree that the Great Commission charges us as disciples of Christ to go into all the world and preach the gospel, that all men are born sinners and stand in need of the regenerating and saving work of God, and that they need to be baptized with water into the name of the triune God of Scripture and brought into his church. Where we disagree is over the meaning and significance of baptism and who is to receive it. Neither of us believes that baptism itself saves anyone, whether infant or adult. The supernatural grace of God must bring sinners to repentance and faith—they must be born again!

A Summary of the Biblical Case for Infant Baptism[10]

This book presents the biblical case for baptizing infants within households headed by believing parents. This position can be summarized under five major headings.

1. *Covenant Theology.* Throughout the Bible, God relates to his people by way of a covenant of grace. Covenant theology provides the basic framework for rightly interpreting Scripture.
2. *Continuity of the Covenant of Grace.* The Bible teaches one and the same way of salvation in both the Old and the New Testaments, despite some different outward requirements.[11]
3. *Continuity of the People of God.* Since there is one covenant of grace between God and man, there is one continuous people of God (the church) in the Old and New Testaments.
4. *Continuity of the Covenant Signs.* Baptism is the sign of the covenant in the New Testament, just as circumcision was the sign of the covenant in the Old Testament.
5. *Continuity of Households.* Whole households are included in God's redemptive covenant.

God has always condescended to relate to humanity through covenantal[12] relationships. These covenants are relationships between a superior (God) and an inferior (man). All such covenants are gracious in character since the creature is not in a position to demand anything from his Creator. Even God's creation covenant with Adam was gracious. After man's fall into sin, God's covenants with man were not only gracious but also redemptive. Their purpose was to redeem unrighteous people from their sinful rebellion and reconcile them with God. This redemptive plan was established from all eternity by the triune God, each person of the Trinity working in harmony to accomplish the divine purpose.

God revealed his redemptive plan immediately after man's fall. This was the first announcement of the gospel, in which God promised to provide a Redeemer (Gen. 3:15). Other glimpses of this gracious covenant are seen in Genesis. For example, God dealt with Noah and his household in a covenant that promised to preserve mankind. The gracious plan of God was formally revealed in God's covenant with Abraham, in which he promised to bless the believer Abraham (Gen. 12 and 17). Abraham believed God's promise to send a Redeemer, and God counted Abraham's faith as righteousness—that is, he was justified by faith alone. As a result of Abraham's righteousness, received by faith, God entered into an everlasting covenant with him and gave him a sign and seal of that covenant—circumcision. God required Abraham not only to receive this covenant sign for himself, but also to apply it to all those in his household, including his children.

The covenant sign was not an indication that those who received it were regenerated. Nor did it mean that they would necessarily be regenerated in the future. Rather, the covenant sign was God's indication that its recipients were *set apart* for his special blessing and use. They therefore stood in need of cleansing, regeneration, and justification. The benefits of the covenant were to be appropriated by faith in the promised Redeemer. To be included in this gracious covenant meant to be an heir of the promise (i.e., one who should lay claim to the Redeemer). A child of the covenant had available all the benefits and privileges of this covenant, including salvation. Yet this same child of the covenant, failing to appropriate these benefits by faith, became a covenant breaker and received God's covenant judgment instead of his covenant blessing.

God's gracious covenant is apparent throughout the Bible. He administered his covenant of grace in different ways at different times, as seen in his relations with Adam, Noah, Abraham, Moses, David, and Jesus.[13] More and more of God's redemptive plan unfolded through history until the final revelation of the covenant of grace was displayed in the new covenant. The new covenant is but a new—though more glorious—administration of the same covenant of grace. The people of God throughout all ages are one and the same people, and they are saved in the same way—they are justified by faith. They worship the same God, have the same ethical standards, trust in the same Redeemer, and have the same Holy Spirit.

Significant changes are made in the new covenant, but only changes that God explicitly made himself. Baptism is one

of several administrative changes. Under the older administrations of the covenant of grace, circumcision was the sign
and seal of covenant admission. Under the final administration of the covenant of grace (the new covenant), water baptism has replaced circumcision as the sign of covenant
admission. The form of the covenant sign has changed (from
circumcision to baptism), yet the spiritual significance of both
forms is essentially the same—both are signs and seals of the
righteousness that is by faith.

The children of believers were always included in the
covenant of grace under the older covenant administrations.
In deference to this established biblical pattern, we must
assume that, apart from explicit biblical warrant to the contrary, the children of believers are still included in the covenant of grace. The grounds remain the same. There is no
teaching in the Bible excluding the children of believers (or
any others in the believer's household) from baptism. We are
therefore obligated to maintain the long-standing practice of
including believers' children in the covenant of grace.

This continuity of the covenant of grace, of the church,
and of the covenant signs provides the primary biblical basis
for baptizing infants of believers. There are also other evidences
in the pages of Scripture that support the truth of infant baptism. Nevertheless, *the foundation of the argument consists of the
unified covenant of grace evident in the Scriptures of the Old and
New Testaments.*

An Open Mind

As you consider the biblical case for infant baptism presented
in this book, I ask you to maintain an open mind and heart
and a willingness to consider a new position. Such openness is
usually difficult for us since it goes against our own pride to
consider whether we may be wrong about anything. We would
do well to consider the advice of Charles Spurgeon, a great
Baptist preacher, as he admonished his listeners while speaking of God's election of sinners to salvation.

Lay aside your prejudices: listen calmly, listen dispassionately: hear what Scripture says; and when you receive the truth, if God should be pleased to reveal and manifest it to your souls, do not be ashamed to confess it. To confess you were wrong yesterday, is only to acknowledge that you are a little wiser today; and instead of being a reflection on yourself, it is an honor to your judgment, and shows that you are improving in the knowledge of the truth. Do not be ashamed to learn, and to cast aside your old doctrines and views, but to take up that which you may more plainly see to be in the Word of God. But if you do not see it to be here in the Bible, whatever I may say, or whatever authorities I may plead, I beseech you, as you love your souls, reject it; and if from this pulpit you ever hear things contrary to this Sacred Word, remember that the Bible must be the first, and God's minister must lie underneath it. We must not stand on the Bible to preach, but we must preach with the Bible above our heads.[14]

NOTES

1. The term *paedobaptist* simply means "child baptizer." The word *Reformed* has reference to the historic Protestant Reformation and the covenantal theology that emerged from that movement. The word may be used in a broad sense, as in the phrase "Reformed Christians," or in a more restricted sense, as in "Reformed paedobaptists." Used together, the terms *Reformed* and *paedobaptist* distinguish those who practice infant baptism because of their covenant theology from others who practice infant baptism for different theological reasons (such as Roman Catholics).
2. For a discussion of the meaning of the word *sacrament,* and the various views taken, see Pierre Ch. Marcel, *The Biblical Doctrine of Infant Baptism* (1953; reprint, Cambridge: James Clarke, 1981).
3. Francis A. Schaeffer, *How Should We Then Live? The Rise and Decline of Western Thought and Culture* (Old Tappan, N.J.: Fleming H. Revell, 1976), 20.
4. John Brown, *Sayings and Discourses of Christ,* rev. ed. (1852; reprint, Winona Lake, Ind.: Alpha Publications, 1967), 1:501.

5. I want to be clear from the beginning that I am in *no way* arguing for the idea that baptism itself has the power to regenerate a person (*baptismal regeneration*) or the idea that we automatically assume that a baptized person will be regenerated (*presumptive regeneration*), nor any form of sacerdotalism! The term "sacerdotalism" has reference to the belief that priests are indispensable mediators between God and man, necessary for the dispensing of God's grace to men.

6. The assumption here is that we are working with fellow Christians who desire to know the truth, i.e., people of proven Christian character whom we seek to persuade and not destroy in the process.

7. The straw man fallacy is an informal logical fallacy. It occurs most often when a person does not like a certain view, and he bases his objection to it on false or exaggerated assumptions as to its nature or consequences. In other words, he carelessly or intentionally misrepresents the position with which he disagrees in order to refute it more easily. It is, therefore, a way of bearing false witness against our neighbor.

8. John Calvin, *Letters of John Calvin,* ed. Jules Bonnet (New York: Burt Franklin, 1972), 2:252.

9. William L. Lumpkin, *Baptist Confessions of Faith* (Valley Forge, Pa.: Judson, 1983), 236. The Congregationalists also adopted the Westminster Confession as their own at the Savoy Conference in 1658, with some changes in the doctrine of the church.

10. The position I am arguing for in this book is the baptism of believers and their children, including infants. We could also speak of "household baptism" as embracing both believers and their children.

11. The term *continuity* refers to the unity of the Bible from the Old to the New Testaments.

12. A "covenant" is an oath-bound agreement between two or more persons. Certain promises are made based on the conditions of the agreement being met. Covenants promise blessings for those who keep the conditions of the agreement, and they promise curses for those who fail to meet the conditions.

13. I am using the phrase *covenant of grace* to refer to God's general covenantal plan to redeem sinful people to himself, a plan born in the eternal counsel of the Trinity. This one covenant of grace extends throughout the Bible from Genesis to Revelation and

finds expression in various historical covenants, such as the Adamic, Noahic, Abrahamic, Mosaic, Davidic, and New Covenants. For a more complete discussion of the historical development of the covenant of grace, see O. Palmer Robertson, *The Christ of the Covenants* (Phillipsburg, N.J.: Presbyterian and Reformed, 1980).

14. Charles H. Spurgeon, *The New Park Street Pulpit* (Pasadena, Tex.: Pilgrim Publications, 1975), 311.

CHAPTER 2

The Pivotal Point: How Should We Interpret the Bible?

KEN JACKSON AND BILL YORK are both in the lumber business. Mr. Jackson owns a lumber mill, and he supplies Mr. York with lumber for his retail building supply business. The two men began doing business with each other in 1942, when they drew up a contract and agreed on many details that would govern their business relationship—details such as markup, terms of payment, return policy, discounts, credit, method of shipment, penalties, etc. By 1965, however, new opportunities presented themselves. Mr. York wanted to vastly expand his retail business into a national franchise. He went to talk to Mr. Jackson about supplying his stores with lumber. Both men realized their contract would have to be changed to address these new business circumstances.

BILL: Ken, we've had a great business relationship over the years. I'm planning to expand my retail operation to cover the entire country. Would you be interested in expanding your mill to supply my stores?

KEN: It sounds like a great opportunity for both of us. Other than needing more capital, what else will this arrangement involve?

BILL: Our contract has worked very well for both of us over the past twenty-three years, but we'll need to change it to address the new areas that such an expansion will involve.

KEN: What changes do you have in mind?

BILL: I've looked into it, and one area we will need to address is the method of shipment. We'll need to change it from railcar to motor freight. There's no question motor freight would save both of us time and money. There are several other matters we need to consider changing as well.

KEN: I'm all for that, but how do we go about it? Do we tear up our old contract and start over with a new one?

BILL: No, that won't be necessary. We can simply amend or update our old contract by addressing the particular areas we want to change. Only those areas covered in the amendment will be affected; the rest of the old contract will remain valid. We just need to sign the amendments and the old contract is updated.

KEN: That makes sense. There's no point in starting completely over since our old contract has worked so well for us. I'll have my attorney contact your attorney, and they can hammer out the details of the needed changes. When they get all the bugs out, we'll set up a time when we can both sign it.

BILL: Sounds good to me.

THE QUESTION OF HOW we should interpret the Bible is at the very heart of the baptism debate—indeed, it is the foundational issue. The fundamental question is whether there is a basic continuity or a basic discontinuity between the Old and New Testaments.[1] How we answer this question will inevitably lead, if we are consistent, to specific conclusions on a host of issues.[2] We all have some method of interpreting the Bible, though our approach may not be well thought out or consistently applied.

Each interpretive system must be tested to see if it is both biblically derived and internally consistent. When methods of interpreting Scripture are fabricated artificially, the Bible is made to fit arbitrary constructs.[3] But since the Bible is our only true authority, our interpretive system must flow from the revelation of God as found in the Old and New Testaments. It must grow out of Scripture, and not be forced on Scripture.

Our story above illustrates two major systems of interpretation—the dispensational[4] and the covenantal[5] methods. The dispensational method sees a *basic discontinuity* between the old and the new covenant (or testament), whereas the covenantal method sees a *basic continuity* between the old and new covenants. When Ken asked about the possibility of tearing up the old contract he had with Bill, he was expressing the idea of discontinuity (the dispensational method). Under this interpretation, the new contract may contain some of the same provisions and stipulations as the old contract, but these provisions and stipulations are only valid because the new contract has spelled them out in a new way. Any parallels between the old contract and the new contract are coincidental and not directly related.

Bill took a different approach. He pointed out that such a radical break with the past was not necessary. He recommended a method that emphasized continuity (the covenantal method). There was no need to cancel the old contract that was still valid and good. The partners only needed to amend or update the old contract, making it current and renewing it to address new circumstances. Any new conditions in the amendment supersede all former conditions in the contract addressing the same issue. All other matters addressed in the old contract remain unchanged and valid. There is a vital relationship between the old contract and the revised contract—a basic unity.

The Reformed or Covenantal Method

The Reformed or covenantal method of interpretation sees *a basic continuity between the Old and New Testaments, with the New flowing out of the Old and building on its foundation.* The New Testament offers a greater revelation of God and his redemptive work, but it does not abruptly do away with the Old Testament and start all over. We even find explicit admonition in the New Testament for believers to rely on the authority of the Old Testament. When Jesus said, "Man shall not live on bread alone, but on every word that proceeds out of the mouth of God" (Matt. 4:4), he was quoting from and referring to the Old Testament. Jesus was unequivocal about the fact that his ministry in no way invalidated the Old Testament. He asserted in Matthew 5:17–19,

> Do not think that I came to abolish the Law or the Prophets; I did not come to abolish, but to fulfill. For truly I say to you, until heaven and earth pass away, not the smallest letter or stroke shall pass away from the Law, until all is accomplished. Whoever then annuls one of the least of these commandments, and so teaches others, shall be called least in the kingdom of heaven; but whoever keeps and teaches them, he shall be called great in the kingdom of heaven.

The Bereans were commended for "examining the Scriptures [Old Testament] daily, to see whether these things were so" (Acts 17:11). Even the apostle's teaching had to withstand the scrutiny of the Old Testament. Paul refers to the Old Testament when he says in Romans 15:4, "For whatever was written in earlier times [Old Testament] was written for our instruction." In 1 Corinthians 10:11 we are told, "Now these things happened to them as an example, and they were written [Old Testament] for our instruction, upon whom the ends of the ages have come." And again we read approvingly of the new covenant use of the Old Testament Scriptures in 2 Timothy 3:15–17.

> From childhood you have known the sacred writings [Old Testament] which are able to give you the wis-

dom that leads to salvation through faith which is in
Christ Jesus. All Scripture [Old Testament] is inspired
by God and profitable for teaching, for reproof, for
correction, for training in righteousness; that the man
of God may be adequate, equipped for every good work.

Besides these passages, Christ and the writers of the New
Testament repeatedly quote from and apply the Old Testament Scriptures to New Testament believers.[6] The New Testament does not set aside the Old Testament. It relies on and
emphasizes the continued validity of the Old Testament for
God's people under the new covenant.

Both the Old and the New Testament interpret one
another. The Reformed principle known as "the analogy of
faith" (that Scripture interprets Scripture) is our guiding interpretive principle. It emphasizes the unity of Scripture,
while allowing for some change where new biblical revelation calls for it. According to covenant theology, the teachings and practices of the Old Testament are still valid and
required for believers in the new covenant era unless God
has revealed in Scripture some change in the use, form, or
application of his previous revelation.

God alone may exercise the prerogative to amend his
Word. In other words, Christians may not arbitrarily declare
any portion of God's Word void, including any portion of the
Old Testament. Any claim for change between the old covenant and the new covenant must be validated by further revelation of God as found in the Scriptures themselves. Both the
Old and the New Testament are to direct the belief and practice of the new covenant believer.

The Dispensational or Baptistic Method

While some Baptists have sought to defend their view of baptism with a covenantal method of interpretation,[7] most Baptists have not taken this approach. Over against the covenantal
approach, the dispensational method of interpretation empha-

sizes *the discontinuity between the Old and New Testaments.* According to this view, while the New Testament often draws from principles in the Old Testament, it is nevertheless a complete replacement of the Old Testament, thus rendering the old covenant invalid.[8] The new covenant believer's starting point is the New Testament, distinct and separate from the Old, and therefore the believer derives all his understanding of the Christian faith from the New Testament alone. The only things carried over from the Old Testament are those things which are explicitly repeated in the New Testament; any other Old Testament teaching is not applicable to the New Testament believer.

The dispensational method of interpretation has divided the Bible into two separate books. These are often portrayed as being substantially different, if not in outright opposition to one another. References are sometimes made to "the God of the Old Testament" being in some ways different from "the God of the New Testament." Such a dividing of the Bible speaks against the essential unchangeableness and unity of God.

R. J. Rushdoony identifies some of the roots of this historical development in eighteenth- and nineteenth-century America:

> Whereas earlier the Puritans had seen the whole Bible as the binding word of God, now, as Jay Fliegelman has noted in *Prodigals and Pilgrims* (1982), "'The Bible' was slowly becoming identified with the New Testament alone." From 1777 to 1800, there were only 33 American editions of the whole Bible, but nearly 80 separate printings of the New Testament. This was a break with the Puritan love of the whole word of God. . . .
>
> The Bible was now seen as a divided book, and, by implication, God was divided and in conflict with Himself. God had one plan of salvation for the Jews, and another for the Christians. . . .
>
> The believer, in his devotional life, was encouraged to concentrate on the New Testament, and the Psalms.

Alexander Campbell attacked the law and called for "New Testament Christianity." Such thinking was seeping into all churches, although Southern Presbyterians resisted it until 1869. The church was abandoning the Bible of Jesus Christ. . . .

Because the other churches stressed the continuity between circumcision and infant baptism, the Baptists attacked the validity of this continuity by denying the continuity between the Old and the New Testaments. Instead of a renewed covenant in Christ with a new Israel of God, a new chosen people, the Baptists insisted on two covenants of differing characteristics.[9]

The Importance of Biblical Continuity

This dividing of the Bible and the covenants of God is unwarranted. We might as well sever a tree from its roots and expect it to survive. The Old and New Testaments are tied together and interdependent. The Old Testament needs the New Testament and the New Testament needs the Old Testament to be properly interpreted and understood. No matter where we start our study of a biblical doctrine, we must consider it in light of the entire Bible.

We must reject any demand that we begin our study of any doctrine with the New Testament alone. This is true for two important reasons. First, the New Testament can be interpreted properly only in the context of the Old Testament. Both the Old Testament text itself and the culture it produced provide the foundation for understanding how those who first received the New Testament would have understood its teaching. God has preserved an inspired, written record of both the history of redemption and the historical experiences of his people. These are not minor points that may be overlooked or brushed aside if we are to come to a right understanding of any doctrine. No fact (or verse) of Scripture is isolated from any other fact—they are all related and have an impact on one another. Therefore, we may not rush to the New Testament, concordance in hand, and presume that we have all the tools and information necessary to reach an accurate conclusion about any doctrine.

A second reason why we should not start with the New Testament is that the doctrines of the New Testament have their roots in the Old Testament. When we read in Galatians 3:29 that we are "Abraham's offspring" and "heirs according to promise," we are immediately driven to Genesis to gain understanding. When we read in Philippians 3:3 that "we are the true circumcision," we must go to the Old Testament to discover what circumcision was and what function it performed. When we read in Romans 15:8 that Christ came "to confirm the promises given to the fathers," or in Ephesians 2:12 that the Gentiles were "excluded from the commonwealth of Israel, and strangers to the covenants of promise," it is only in the Old Testament that we discover the foundation for these teachings.

How did the Jews understand the baptism of John in John 3:25? What were the various baptisms of Hebrews 9:10? Why was circumcision of the heart in Colossians 2:11–12 represented by baptism? What represented circumcision of the heart in the Old Testament? It would be useless to try to answer these basic questions without turning to the Old Testament. The New Testament similarly drives us immediately to the Old Testament when we try to understand the doctrines of creation, sin, redemption, the sacrifice of Christ, the Atonement, the priesthood, the eldership, church discipline, the Lord's Supper, marriage, divorce, households, covenants, judgment, heaven, and much more.

In a letter to his son in 1850, we see an example of how C. C. Jones applied this principle of biblical interpretation to the question of capital punishment. This same principle of continuity must be brought to bear on all other doctrinal questions, including baptism. Jones advised his son:

> The fallacy of your young friend on the capital punishment question, so far as the Scriptures are concerned,

lies in setting the New Testament over and above the Old, whereas both are equally the Word of God, equally authoritative, and form *one* perfect revelation, one perfect rule of faith and practice. They are not in any respect antagonistic, but consonant, and mutually support the one the other. Nothing is set aside in the Old Testament in and by the New save the types and shadows and ceremonial laws, all which find their fulfillment in our Lord and saviour Jesus Christ and expire, as the lawyers would say, by the statute of their own limitation. But all the laws of God that embody our duties to God and men, whether socially or civilly, remain ever in force. These laws are recognized in the New Testament, but not repeated *in extenso,* there being no necessity for it. . . . The New Testament is built up out of and upon the Old, and is not contrary to it in any thing whatever. It ever recognizes and then supports the Old.

Another fallacy of your young friend is that we are not bound to do anything but what we are distinctly commanded in so many words by the New Testament to do. You perceive at once that this principle cannot be admitted without involving us in many difficulties. This fallacy grows out of the first and falls with it. All that is necessary is for the New Testament to acknowledge the Old, and the two be united in *one* perfect revelation. Neither is complete without the other. . . .

I need not proceed any further. You can manage the controversy now, I think, with this little help.[10]

The dispensational method of isolating the New Testament from the Old Testament, as though we may determine any doctrine in its proper relation to redemptive history with the New Testament alone, is dangerous and misguided. The problem with this dispensational method is not so much that it starts with the New Testament, since the New Testament immediately points us to the Old Testament. The real problem posed by this method is that it not only wants to start with the New Testament but also wants to stop with the New Testament and settle the issue with the New Testament alone. We must not forget that all Scripture—including the Old Testament—is profitable for doctrine (2 Tim. 3:16). Starting and ending with the whole Bible is the only sure way to arrive at sound doctrinal positions. The dispensational system does not adequately account for the unity of the Bible.[11]

Given the unchangeable character of God, there can be no question about the principle of continuity in his revelation (the Bible). Continuity and unity should be presumed over discontinuity. Who, but God alone, may presume to change what God has said? When it comes to Scripture, only God is permitted to say what is in fact new about the new covenant. As Greg Bahnsen has explained, "Everything God has said should be that by which man lives (Matt. 4:4), not simply those things which God has spoken *twice* (and in the right places). We must live by *every* Scripture unless God explains otherwise."[12]

This basic unity of God and his revelation is seen in the fact that God has, from the beginning, dealt with humanity in terms of redemptive covenants. God has had one plan from the start to redeem sinners. He has pursued and brought that plan to pass in a smooth and unbroken fashion. God has continuously unfolded, through more and more revelation, his redemptive plan for man and the world.

The Concept of the Covenant

If we are to rightly understand the Bible, we must understand the concept of a covenant. A covenant, when formed between a superior and an inferior, is a "conditional promise." A reward is promised, on the condition of obedience, and punishment is threatened for disobedience. For example, "Whosoever believes shall be saved, whosoever believeth not shall be damned."[13] The covenant is not only law, but also grace. It is only by the ill-deserved favor of God (i.e., grace) that he chooses to covenant with sinful men.[14] Another writer adds to this definition that a covenant is "*a bond in blood sovereignly administered.* When God enters a covenant relationship with men, he sovereignly institutes a life-and-death bond. A covenant is a bond in blood, or a bond of life and death, sovereignly administered."[15]

We should, therefore, understand a covenant between God and man to be *a conditional promise, sealed by blood, sovereignly administered by God, with blessings for those who obey the conditions of the covenant and curses for those who disobey its conditions.*

God has always been a covenant-keeping God (Deut. 7:9). There is even a covenantal relationship among the three persons of the Godhead, in which the triune God purposed to save sinful men from their fallen condition. Charles Spurgeon describes this eternal covenantal arrangement as follows:

> There was a time before all time, when there was no day but the Ancient of Days, when all that existed was the Lord, who is all in all: then the sacred Three entered into covenant, in mutual agreement, for a sublime end. Man sinning, the Son of God shall be the surety. Christ shall bear the result of man's offence; he shall vindicate the law of God, and make Jehovah's name more glorious than ever it has been. The Second Person of the divine Unity was pledged to come, and take up the nature of men, and so become the firstborn among many brethren, and lift up a fallen race, and to save a number that no man can number.[16]

The various historical covenantal relationships with Adam, Noah, Abraham, Moses, David, and Jesus represent the outworking of God's redemptive plan.[17] These covenants unfold in time to reveal the promised Messiah. This promise of a Redeemer, revealed first in Genesis 3:15, develops and matures until it reaches full bloom in the new covenant of Jesus Christ.

The Bible is primarily a record of redemptive history. All other events of history are secondary to this work of redemption. The triune, covenantal God deals with people on the basis of covenants. In the case of the covenant among the three persons of the Godhead, we see a covenant among equals. In the case of God's covenants with men and women, we see a covenant between a superior and inferiors.

God's covenants pertain not only to individuals but also to the various corporate spheres of human life, such as households and society. The dispensational approach emphasizes God's redemptive work on the individual's personal salvation. The covenantal approach recognizes that God, while concerned with individual redemption, in no way neglects the other aspects of life. From the beginning of creation, Scripture reveals God's purpose to redeem man and every area of his life. The household of the believer and its successive generations always play a dominant role in God's redemptive plan.

God entered a gracious covenant with Adam, the first man. In this Adamic covenant, God promised Adam life on the condition of his perfect obedience. Not only did Adam represent himself in this covenant, but all his descendants stood or fell in his obedience or disobedience. The whole human family was embraced by the Adamic covenant, with Adam as its covenantal head. Every man who would ever be born was dealt with by God through the first man Adam—he was every man's representative. Even though they did not yet exist as historical individuals, God thought of them and dealt with them through Adam.[18]

After Adam broke the initial covenant, God quickly moved to establish a new covenant with man—a gracious covenant of redemption, which we call the covenant of grace. This covenant unfolds throughout the Old and New Testaments. It is first seen in the promise of redemption recorded in Genesis 3:15. God declared to the Serpent, "And I will put enmity between you and the woman, and between your seed and her seed; He shall bruise you on the head, and you shall bruise him on the heel." This promise of a Savior culminated in the person and work of Jesus Christ and the declaration of the apostle John in Revelation 21:3, "Behold,

the tabernacle of God is among men, and He shall dwell
among them, and they shall be his people, and God Himself
shall be among them."

   If we inherited the consequences of sin without personally asking for them, why not the promise of redemption
also? All of God's dealings with humanity are in terms of
either his judgment or his grace. His justice demands satisfaction (judgment) when his righteous standards have been
violated. God's grace in Jesus Christ provides the satisfaction
demanded. Therefore, all people either stand on their own—
guilty and under God's wrath—or else they stand within the
bounds of God's covenant of grace, in which he dictates the
"terms of mercy." It is by his covenant that God establishes
the conditions of his promise of mercy and redemption for
sinful men. It is by covenant that God promises a Redeemer.
Outside this covenantal arrangement, man is hopelessly lost
and under God's wrath and judgment.

   Some Baptists have conceded this point of covenantal
continuity. For example, Paul Jewett writes,

> The theological conception sometimes called covenant
> theology which undergirds the Paedobaptist argument
> at this point, is too grand, too challenging, too persis-
> tent to be ignored with impunity. The dogmatician who
> slights it despises his own reputation. This is perhaps
> to concede that the Baptists as a whole have not been
> outstanding theologians; the stream of their rebuttal
> has run so thin at this juncture that only the hollow
> eyes of predisposition could fail to see its inadequacy
> and judge the counter arguments superior.[19]

And David Kingdon perceptively observes,

> A great deal of Baptist apologetic, so it seems to me, has
> failed to come to terms with the indubitable fact that
> the covenant of grace, although it exhibits diversity of
> administration in the time of promise and in the time

of fulfillment, is none-the-less one covenant. . . . The divisive, atomistic approach of so much contemporary Baptist apologetic is about as effective at this point as a shot-gun against a Sherman tank.[20]

God's covenants are essentially one. The Redeemer, Jesus Christ, is the object of each particular covenantal administration of the one covenant of grace. The apostle Paul gave assurance to the Gentile Christians concerning their relationship to Jewish believers when he said, "There is . . . one Lord, one faith, one baptism, one God and Father of all who is over all and through all and in all" (Eph. 4:4–6). This is the same God who said, "My covenant I will not violate, nor will I alter the utterance of My lips" (Ps. 89:34).

What Does This Have to Do with Infant Baptism?

It cannot be overemphasized how important our interpretive principle is when it comes to understanding and applying Scripture. *This is the pivotal point on which the discussion of baptism or any other doctrine will turn.* In fact, until two people come to some basic agreement about how Scripture is to be interpreted, it is unlikely that they will agree on other matters, including baptism. Our basic interpretive assumptions have everything to do with the conclusions we draw.[21]

To illustrate this important point of interpretive principle, consider how two people would settle a dispute over the length of a room if each of them had a stick that he considered to be exactly one yard long—yet the sticks were of different lengths. How could they ever settle their dispute? The disagreement over which standard of measurement is going to be used must be settled first. Likewise, our rules of interpretation must be established and agreed upon before we can have any hope of settling doctrinal disputes. Have you considered what method you use to interpret the Bible? What principle guides you in this most important task—basic discontinuity or basic continuity? Dispensational or covenantal?

The covenantal interpretive principle provides a consistent and biblical method for interpreting the Bible. It is from this covenantal position that I will deal with the question of who should be baptized. Given the covenantal principle of continuity, the burden of proof rests with those who claim that the practice of including infants in God's gracious covenant has been changed. Those who hold that infants should receive the covenant sign of baptism do so (among other reasons) on the basis of assumed continuity from the Old Testament to the New.

A covenantal method of interpretation, if consistently held, will lead to an understanding and acceptance of baptizing the infants of believers as members of the covenant of grace. The dispensational method of interpretation, if consistently held, will inevitably lead to an individualistic and baptistic understanding of baptism. Has God had one plan of redemption (covenantal), or has he had more than one plan (dispensational)? This question must be answered if we are to go on in our study of baptism.

NOTES

1. By the terms *continuity* and *discontinuity* I refer to the degree to which the Old Testament continues in an uninterrupted way to be valid or have application in the New Testament.
2. For example: the abiding validity of the ethical demands of the Old Testament law, the nature of God's covenantal relationship with man, eschatology, baptism, and the nature of the church.
3. A "construct" is a method of arranging ideas into a systematic form. While such systems are unavoidable, they should not be arbitrary. Our system of biblical interpretation must come from Scripture itself.
4. A "dispensation" is a specific period of time. The dispensational method of biblical interpretation holds that there is much variety and change from one biblical era to the next. God deals differently with men in the various dispensations.
5. Covenant theology emphasizes that God relates to men by way of covenants. God has a single, comprehensive plan of redemption extending from Genesis to Revelation. This plan is called

"the covenant of grace." The covenantal method of biblical interpretation maintains that God has dealt with men in the same way throughout history.

6. E.g., 2 Cor. 6:16–18; Rom. 8:36; 9:25–26; 10:6–8, 11, 13, 15; Gal. 4:27; Heb. 8:8–12; 10:30; 13:5; 1 Peter 2:10.

7. For example, David Kingdon's *Children of Abraham* (Cambridge: Carey Publications, 1975) attempts to take a covenantal approach to the question of baptism. Kingdon rightly recognizes the problems with the dispensational defense of the baptistic position, along with many of the strengths of the covenantal arguments. Nevertheless, Kingdon falls short of harmonizing the covenantal and baptistic views. This is the middle ground that I sought to occupy for many years myself.

8. Some Baptists maintain that the moral law expressed in the Old Testament is still valid for New Testament believers. This arbitrary determination is inconsistent with the contention that the old covenant has been replaced by the new covenant.

9. R. J. Rushdoony, *The Roots of Reconstruction* (Vallecito, Calif.: Ross House Books, 1991), 266, 267, 269.

10. Robert Manson Myers, *A Georgian at Princeton* (New York: Harcourt Brace Jovanovich, 1976), 89–90.

11. There may be some protests at this point from those Baptists who do not wholeheartedly embrace the dispensational method and who claim to be covenantal in their theology. However, a person may be generally covenantal in his interpretation of Scripture yet follow a dispensational method at a particular point. Dispensational and covenant theology are mutually exclusive systems of interpretation, and consistency demands one or the other, not a switching from one to the other as it suits the interpreter. For example, some "covenantal Baptists" argue that we may use only the New Testament to settle the issue of who should be baptized. But to exclude any part of the Bible from our understanding of any topic reflects a dispensational method, and this runs counter to covenant theology.

12. Greg L. Bahnsen, *Theonomy in Christian Ethics*, 2d ed. (Phillipsburg, N.J.: Presbyterian and Reformed, 1984), 184.

13. A. A. Hodge, *Evangelical Theology* (1890; reprint, Carlisle, Pa.: Banner of Truth, 1976), 166, 172.

14. John Frame, *The Doctrine of the Knowledge of God* (Phillipsburg, N.J.: Presbyterian and Reformed, 1987), 12.

15. O. Palmer Robertson, *The Christ of the Covenants* (Phillipsburg, N.J.: Presbyterian and Reformed, 1980), 4.

16. Charles H. Spurgeon, *The Metropolitan Tabernacle Pulpit* 37 (1908): 249 (in a sermon on Ps. 40:6–8), quoted in Roderick Campbell, *Israel and the New Covenant* (Philadelphia: Presbyterian and Reformed, 1954), 25.

17. It cannot be denied that there does exist an eternal, divine provision for the redemption of fallen men, whether one sees it as a formal covenant or not. The redemptive-historical covenants are clearly based on a transcendent plan, as implied in these passages: John 6:38–40; 10:18, 36; 17:4, 6, 24; Rom. 16:25–26; Eph. 1:3–6; 3:11; Phil. 2:6–8; 2 Tim. 1:9; Titus 1:2; 1 Peter 1:19–20.

18. Cornelius Van Til, *The Defense of the Faith,* 3d ed. (Philadelphia: Presbyterian and Reformed, 1967), 190.

19. Paul King Jewett, "Baptism (Baptist View)," in *Encyclopedia of Christianity,* 1:541, quoted in David Kingdon, *Children of Abraham,* 20.

20. Kingdon, *Children of Abraham,* 20–21.

21. This assumes that we are consistent with what we profess to be our basic interpretive principle. People often attempt to synthesize principles in order to justify their precommitment to a particular belief. Thus they end up as, e.g., "theistic evolutionists," "Calvinistic Arminians," or "covenantal Baptists."

CHAPTER 3

The Covenants of Promise: The Bud of Redemption

MR. DAVIDSON, a very wealthy man, had one son, who was faithful to his father and brought him delight. Mr. Davidson intended for his son to inherit all he had, so he called his son in to speak to him.

FATHER: Son, I'm pleased to have you as my son. You've been faithful to me and our household, and you've proved yourself to be a responsible young man.

SON: Thank you, Father. You make it easy to be such a son. Your instruction and love have served me well.

FATHER: I have asked you to come and see me today because I have something to tell you and something to give you. God has been gracious to me and has blessed the labor of my hands. He has caused me to prosper greatly. In fact, my wealth is immense. It is my desire that you, as my son, should inherit all I possess. This is what I wanted to tell you about. Now, as a token of my promise to give you all that I have, and in the expectation of your continued faithfulness, I want to give you this ring. You should wear it as a continual reminder of your promised inheritance. Indeed, the ring itself is a part of the inheritance. In the days ahead, when you may be tempted to grow discouraged in life, the ring will remind you of my promise to you and provide a hope for the future. I love you, Son, so persevere to the end.

SON: I love you too, Father, and I shall wear this ring forever and always remember your promise to me.

After many years passed, Mr. Davidson died. His son inherited all his wealth. The son kept the ring that his father had given to him as a perpetual reminder of his father's faithfulness to his promise.

IN THIS STORY, the ring that Mr. Davidson gave to his son was symbolic of the promise of an inheritance that was to come. It was itself a part of the inheritance, though very small in comparison to the full estate. Mr. Davidson attached meaning to the ring, just as God attached meaning to various symbols of his promise to send a Redeemer to his people. Whenever the symbol was viewed, it served as a reminder of what was promised. Even after the promise was fulfilled, Mr. Davidson's son continued to wear the ring fondly, rather than discarding it.

When the full inheritance came, the ring's significance changed, becoming a symbolic reminder of what his father had promised. Though the ring's worth was surpassed by the full inheritance, it remained a prized possession. Instead of replacing the ring, the inheritance heightened the son's appreciation of what the ring had symbolized all along. What once spoke of his father's promise, now served to remind the son of his father's proven faithfulness.

In the covenants made with Adam, Noah, Abraham, Moses, and David, God provided tokens of his promise of a Redeemer who would be finally revealed in the new covenant. When the promise was fulfilled, the tokens were not discarded. They did, however, take on a different significance and use. Together, the covenants combined to form God's unified plan of redemptive history.

The Unity of the Covenants

Are God's various covenants a succession of separate, unrelated covenants? Does he end one covenant and then replace it with a new one? Or, do the covenants build on one another, unfolding God's redemptive plan, little by little, until his whole purpose is revealed? In other words, has God had one single plan of redemption for all his people in all times, or has he had multiple plans that address different people in different times?

The covenantal view sees one unified plan of redemption that embraces every area of life—individuals, families, and society. The dispensational view envisions various plans, including different goals and people. The Scriptures support the covenantal position. This point is emphasized by O. Palmer Robertson.

> The cumulative evidence of the Scriptures points definitely toward the unified character of the biblical covenants. God's multiple bonds with his people ultimately unite into a single relationship. Particular details of the covenants may vary. A definite line of progression may be noted. Yet the covenants of God are one.[1]

There is but one covenant of grace—one conditional promise of redemption—that runs throughout all Scripture and redemptive history. Within this one covenant of grace there are a variety of administrations.[2] These various administrations are seen in the Adamic covenant, the Noahic covenant, the Abrahamic covenant, the Mosaic covenant, the Davidic covenant, and the new covenant.[3] John Calvin recognized this gradual development of God's redemptive plan.

The Lord held to this orderly plan in administering the covenant of his mercy: as the day of full revelation approached with the passing of time, the more he increased each day the brightness of its manifestation. Accordingly, at the beginning when the first promise of salvation was given to Adam it glowed like a feeble spark. Then, as it was added to, the light grew in fullness, breaking forth increasingly and shedding its radiance more widely. At last—when all the clouds were dispersed—Christ, the Sun of Righteousness, fully illuminated the whole earth.[4]

Each of the covenantal administrations built upon and expanded the revelation of the one redemptive promise. In Ephesians 2:12 we are told that the Gentiles were "strangers to the covenants of promise." Notice that Paul refers to only one promise but to a plurality of covenants that administered that one promise.[5]

The covenant of grace is like a constitution, in that it must be administered. There is one covenant (or constitution), but there are various administrations over time.[6] Covenantal administrations are similar to the various presidential administrations in the United States, each of which administers the one U.S. Constitution. The Constitution transcends various presidential administrations. Although certain amendments may be lawfully made to the Constitution under a particular administration, the one Constitution remains in place. We do not see a brand-new constitution each time the administration changes.

The question of whether there is one single covenant of grace, extending through both the Old and the New Testaments, is central to the baptism debate. Calvin saw that if infant baptism were to be overturned, then the continuity of the old covenant with the new covenant would have to be disproved. The famous English Baptist John Gill went so far as to deny that the Abrahamic covenant was a covenant of grace! Gill said, "Now that this covenant was not the pure covenant of grace, in distinction from the covenant of works, but rather a covenant of works, will soon be proved; and if so, then the main ground of infant baptism is taken away." He argued that the covenant of grace mentioned in Galatians 3 refers to God's covenant with Abraham in Genesis 12, but not to his "covenant of works" in Genesis 17.[7] The obvious teaching of the continuity of the old and the new covenants has lead some dispensationalists and Baptists to posit a "second" covenant with Abraham, one that better confirms their system of thought.[8]

But the Bible is unified in its presentation of God's one redemptive plan. *The Lord has been steadfast in bringing his plan to pass in a smooth and unbroken fashion, showing his redemptive concern for individuals, families, and society.* Since each of these areas of human life was disastrously affected by the Fall, God purposed to redeem every affected area in a glorious way. Each covenantal administration played an essential role in bringing about the magnificent climax of God's plan to redeem sinners.

Comprehensive Redemption

Though God purposed to redeem individuals, his plan included much more. He also laid claim to their households and societies. How could the redeemed individual prosper without a family and a world brought under the influences of redemption? We must ask, Under what conditions does the individual believer prosper? (1) With or without a civil government? With a godly or ungodly civil government? (2) With or without a church? With a godly or ungodly church?[9] (3) With or without a family? With a godly or ungodly family?

The answers to these questions are obvious—godly institutions serve the redeemed individual. God is therefore concerned to redeem every area of man's life.

From the time of man's creation, God has revealed his concern for man, his family, and his society. He has provided laws to govern each of these, thereby demonstrating their necessity and importance. Any theology that fails to embrace every aspect of human life also fails to appreciate the comprehensive nature of God's one redemptive plan. God loves not only the individual believer, but also the believer's household. And he is concerned to see the believer's society brought under the influence of redemption. His redemptive plan extends "far as the curse is found." An examination of the historic covenants demonstrates this concern.

The Adamic Covenant

God demonstrated this comprehensive concern for creation in the covenant he made with Adam before the Fall. The Lord gave Adam a family to rule over, and he placed him in the Garden of Eden, with rules to administer that society. Adam represented not only himself, but also his household and the world. In fact, Adam stood as the head of the whole human race.

When Adam failed to keep this gracious covenant with God, it was not only he himself who suffered the consequences but also his entire household and society. Adam was the federal head of all who were under his authority in this covenant with God. Because Adam was a covenant breaker, God cursed Adam, his wife, their children, and the whole earth (Gen. 3:14–19).

Having violated the first covenant with God, Adam came under the curse of that covenant. Nevertheless, God was pleased, even in the midst of pronouncing the curse upon Adam and his descendants, to establish a new covenant with him and to promise a Redeemer. The covenant of grace was immediately put in place to provide redemption for sinful men. We see in the first promise of the gospel (Gen. 3:15) an anticipation of both the method by which redemption would be accomplished and the mystery of its application. This promise will tie in with all subsequent administrations of the covenant of grace.[10] It is this promised "seed of the woman," the Lord Jesus Christ, who will ultimately crush the head of the Serpent and redeem sinful men, their households, and their society.

This spark of a promise, made to Adam and Eve, will grow into a blazing fire of glory in the new covenant.

The Noahic Covenant

Next, God reestablished his gracious covenant with Noah (Gen. 8:20–22; 9:1–17), who "found favor in the eyes of the LORD" (Gen. 6:8). This new administration of God's covenant was built on his previous covenant with Adam and repeated many of the original covenantal terms (Gen. 9:1–3). God demonstrated his redemptive purpose by directing his electing love toward one man *and his family*. Righteous Noah (Gen. 6:9) was preserved, along with his entire household: "But I will establish My covenant with you; and you shall enter the ark—you and your sons and your wife, and your sons' wives with you" (Gen. 6:18).

God saved them from his judgment and baptized them in the ark (1 Peter 3:20–21).[11] In the Flood, God redeemed not only righteous Noah but also his family and the world. What basis does Scripture give for preserving Noah and his family? Genesis 7:1 provides the reason: "Then the LORD said to Noah, 'Enter the ark, you and all your household; for you [singular] alone I have seen to be righteous before Me in this time.'" The basis for Noah's entering the ark was that he alone was righteous. Noah's family also entered the ark on the basis of Noah's righteousness. Throughout his dealings with Noah, God included Noah's household as part of the covenant relationship (cf. Gen. 7:1, 7, 13, 23; 8:16, 18; 9:9, 12).

The redemptive covenants of God provide a comprehensive worldview for his people, embracing the totality of their lives.[12] God is not concerned only with the narrow (though important) purpose of saving individual souls. He also extends his redemptive purview to include the institutions where individual men must live and be nurtured. The covenant with Noah must be characterized as a future-oriented covenant, as God not only reestablished the covenants made with Adam, but also promised to preserve mankind from total destruction (Gen. 9:15), thus laying the covenantal groundwork for his future redemptive work. Every time we see a rainbow in the sky—the covenant sign—we are reassured that God's covenant with Noah remains in effect.

The Abrahamic Covenant

The Lord continued to unfold his gracious plan of redemption, first revealed in the covenants made with Adam and Noah, when he called Abram (later renamed Abraham) out from Ur of the Chaldees (Gen. 15:7). With Abraham we see the great promise of a Redeemer clearly set forth in what has been characterized as the "covenant of promise." The covenant that God made with Abraham in Genesis 17 demonstrates once again that his one redemptive purpose includes the individual believer, his household, and society. His covenantal promises embrace every aspect of the believer's existence, both internal and external. We read in verses 1–8,

> Now when Abram was ninety-nine years old, the LORD appeared to Abram and said to him, "I am God Almighty; walk before Me, and be blameless. And I will establish My covenant between Me and you, and I will multiply you exceedingly." And Abram fell on his face, and God talked with him, saying, "As for Me, behold, My covenant is with you, and you shall be the father of a multitude of nations. No longer shall your name be called Abram, but your name shall be Abraham; for I will make you the father of a multitude of nations. And I will make you exceedingly fruitful, and I will make nations of you, and kings shall come forth from you. And I will establish My covenant between Me and you and your descendants after you throughout their generations for an everlasting covenant, to be God to you and to your descendants after you. And I will give to you and to your descendants after you, the land of your sojournings, all the land of Canaan, for an everlasting possession; and I will be their God."

This is the great, everlasting covenant of promise made to Abraham, the "father of all who believe" (Rom. 4:11). Abraham believed God and "it was reckoned to him as righteousness" (Rom. 4:3). God then gave Abraham a sign and seal of that "righteousness which is by faith" (Rom. 9:30)[13] by calling for his outward circumcision (Rom. 4:11).

Again, God was concerned not only with the individual believer, Abraham, but also with his household and his society. Abraham was to apply the covenant sign of "the righteousness which is by faith" not only to himself but also to his entire household, including newborn infants (Gen. 17:10–14).

This familial aspect of the covenant was necessary for the complete success of the redemption of man. When the question is asked, "For what purpose did God choose Abraham?" we find that the answer in Genesis 18:19 is directed toward the essential work of godly instruction in Abraham's household: "For I have chosen him, in order that he may command his children and his household after him to keep the way of the Lord by doing righteousness and justice; in order that the Lord may bring upon Abraham what He has spoken about him."

The Lord was concerned with the faithfulness of Abraham and also that of his household. In fact, the spiritual instruction of the family is one of the primary duties of believers in the covenant of grace. Notice that the promise made to Abraham was contingent upon the genuine faithfulness of successive generations. This was no mere externalism; such would not be acceptable. Rather, God demanded genuine faithfulness from all those who were bound by his covenant with Abraham—Abraham's entire household. The sign and seal of this demand of God was circumcision (Gen. 17:14). When people perform any ceremony apart from genuine faith in God, the Lord finds the exercise offensive. Likewise, when people profess faith and yet ignore rituals that God has prescribed, he finds that obnoxious.[14]

The Abrahamic covenant provided the foundation for the covenants that followed it. The covenants made with Moses, David, and Christ were developments of this basic covenant of

promise (cf. 1 Chron. 16:15–17; Ps. 105:8–15). The Mosaic
covenant (Ex. 19:5–6; 24:3) was an addendum to the Abrahamic covenant. The Davidic covenant conformed to the Mosaic
(2 Sam. 7; 23:5; 2 Chron. 6:14–17; 21:7; Pss. 89:3–4; 132:11–
18). Finally, Christ came to "confirm the promises given to the
fathers" (Rom. 15:8). The fundamental promise of the covenants is repeated throughout Scripture: "I will be your God,
and you shall be my people" (cf. Ex. 19:5; Deut. 4:20; Jer.
31:1, 33; Heb. 8:10; 1 Peter 2:9). This will be accomplished
through the single "seed of Abraham," who is Christ (Gal. 3:16).

The Mosaic Covenant

God distinguished a people for himself in his covenant with
Abraham. He then proceeded to develop and bring to pass his
promised redemption. In each expansion of God's redemptive revelation, we see an emphasis on continuity and unity
with each of the previous covenants. We must not overlook or
minimize this essential unity of the covenants. God's ultimate
purpose has always been clearly before him as he providen-
tially accomplishes the redemption of the fallen world. Instead
of starting over with a brand new covenant, each successive
covenant with Abraham's descendants advances God's original purposes to a greater level of realization.[15]

Some have argued that the Mosaic covenant was a break
with the Abrahamic covenant. On the contrary, it was God remembering his covenant with Abraham that caused him to
redeem his people from their bondage in Egypt. "So God heard
their groaning; and God remembered His covenant with Abraham, Isaac, and Jacob" (Ex. 2:24; cf. also Ex. 6:4–8). The whole
Mosaic covenant was built on the previously sworn promises
of God:

> So keep the words of this covenant to do them, that
> you may prosper in all that you do. You stand today,
> all of you, before the LORD your God: your chiefs, your
> tribes, your elders and your officers, even all the men

of Israel, *your little ones*, your wives, and the alien who is
within your camps, from the one who chops your wood
to the one who draws your water, that you may enter
into the covenant with the LORD your God, and into
His oath which the LORD your God is making with you
today, in order that He may establish you today as His
people and that He may be your God, just as He spoke
to you and as He swore to your fathers, to Abraham,
Isaac, and Jacob. Now not with you alone am I making
this covenant and this oath, but both with those who
stand here with us today in the presence of the LORD
our God and *with those who are not with us here today.*
(Deut. 29:9–15, italics added)

In the Mosaic administration of the covenant of grace,
God's redemptive purpose included individual men, their
households (including the "little ones"), and their society.
Moreover, the covenant was not made just with those who were
present then, but also with those who were not yet born. This
redemption, as in all of God's covenants, was conditioned on
the covenant faithfulness of its members.

Personal salvation is not automatically given to those who
are merely externally circumcised (or baptized). God required
a "circumcised heart" (Deut. 30:6). Anything less than covenant faithfulness brought God's curses rather than his blessings. When people would ask why the Lord had brought
judgment on them, he would reply, "Because they forsook the
covenant of the LORD, the God of their fathers" (Deut. 29:25).

There has certainly been much misunderstanding of the
nature and function of the Mosaic covenant. The Judaizers in
the New Testament turned it into a "covenant of works."[16] The
Mosaic covenant was a part of the covenant of grace, administered by the righteous law of God. Nothing but faithful commitment from the heart was ever acceptable to him, even in the
Mosaic covenant (Deut. 6:4–9). Roderick Campbell, in his book
Israel and the New Covenant, provides a good description of some
of the functions of the Mosaic covenant, which may help us

appreciate and understand this covenant better. Here is a ten-point summary of what he says about the Mosaic covenant:

1. It was designed to bring the Abrahamic promises to fruition.
2. It provided the governmental constitution for the infant nation of Israel.
3. It was a revelation of transcendent truth in visible, audible, and symbolic form. It was "a pattern of things in the heavens," a "shadow of good things to come" (Heb. 9–10).
4. It was a divinely prescribed method and system of worship and fellowship.
5. It was clearly preparatory and tentative. The Old Testament promises a greater prophet than Moses (Deut. 18:15; Mal. 3:1), a greater priest than Aaron (Zech. 6:12–13), a greater king than David or Solomon (Ps. 72), a greater tabernacle and temple (1 Kings 8:27; Isa. 2:2–3), and a greater worship of, and access to, God (Mal. 1:11).
6. The events, laws, actors, objects, and ceremonies of the Mosaic covenant clarify and fix the language of sacred truth, enabling communications.
7. The Mosaic covenant demonstrated the necessity and advantage of a religious covenant community.
8. It provided a panoramic and parabolic preview of redemption.
9. It served as a wall to preserve the knowledge of the true God, as well as a protection of God's people from corrupting influences.
10. It provided a record of inexhaustible instruction, warning, and comfort for all true worshipers of God.[17]

The Mosaic covenant did not do away with the Abrahamic covenant; rather, it was built on the promises made to (Gal. 3:21). The Abrahamic and Mosaic covenants provided both the promises and the directives for God's people to ensure the future success of his one redemptive plan. For generation after generation, the children of those who were faithful to the covenant were preserved and established, but those who were unfaithful to the covenant were cut off from among God's covenant people.

The Davidic Covenant

God's one plan of redemption unfolded in time to reveal more of his purpose as he entered into covenant with David. This new administration of the covenant of grace is described in 2 Samuel 7, which relates how God inaugurated and established his kingdom. The kingship of David prefigured the everlasting kingship of David's descendant—King Jesus.

The unique feature of this Davidic covenant was the establishment of a king over Israel forever. The Lord spoke to David through Nathan, saying, "When your days are complete and you lie down with your fathers, I will raise up your descendant after you, who will come forth from you, and I will establish his kingdom. He shall build a house for My name, and I will establish the throne of his kingdom forever" (vv. 12–13). This prophecy was fulfilled both in Solomon and eventually in Jesus Christ. King David never hesitated to appeal to the previous covenant oaths of God and to apply them to his kingdom.[18] The Davidic covenant specifically identified itself with both the Abrahamic and the Mosaic covenants. For example, David recallee the promises that God had made to Abraham when he sang about the ark being brought to Jerusalem:

> Remember His covenant forever, the word which He commanded to a thousand generations, the covenant which He made with Abraham, and His oath to Isaac. He also confirmed it to Jacob for a statute, to Israel as an everlasting covenant, saying, "To you I will give the land of Canaan, as the portion of your inheritance." (1 Chron. 16:15–18)

David was fully aware of his relationship with the fathers, Abraham, Isaac, and Jacob. He understood that the events of his own generation were the result of God's covenant faithfulness.[19] Even though God made a covenant with David, there is no thought that this annulled the previous covenants. In the context of establishing his covenant with David, the Lord did not sever his previous covenantal relationships with his people. The Lord reminded David, "For I have not dwelt in a house since the day I brought up the sons of Israel from Egypt, even to this day; but I have been moving about in a tent, even in a tabernacle" (2 Sam. 7:6). The covenant promises having been made, David responded to God by remembering God's dealings with his people under the Mosaic covenant, and then by relating this covenant to his own.

> For Thou hast established for Thyself Thy people Israel as Thine own people forever, and Thou, O LORD, hast become their God. Now therefore, O LORD God, the word that Thou hast spoken concerning Thy servant and his house, confirm it forever, and do as Thou hast spoken, that Thy name may be magnified forever, by saying, "The LORD of hosts is God over Israel"; and may the house of Thy servant David be established before Thee. (2 Sam. 7:24–26)

Again, as David was dying and giving his charge to Solomon, he reminded him that the covenant promises that God had made to him rested on the faithful keeping of the law given to Moses.

> And keep the charge of the LORD your God, to walk in His ways, to keep His statutes, His commandments, His ordinances, and His testimonies, according to what is written in the law of Moses, that you may succeed in all that you do and wherever you turn, so that the LORD may carry out His promise which He spoke concerning me, saying, "If your sons are careful of their way,

to walk before Me in truth with all their heart and with all their soul, you shall not lack a man on the throne of Israel." (1 Kings 2:3–4)

David definitely identified his covenant with the Mosaic covenant. We see again that the Lord's covenants embrace the individual believer (David), his household, and his society (Israel). We should also note that mere physical descent from David was not sufficient reason for a descendant to receive covenant blessings. God required, as he always had, covenant faithfulness from the heart. Then, and only then, could covenant blessing be expected and the redemptive promises be fulfilled.

Covenant Continuity

In the Old Testament covenants, the flower bud of redemption swells in anticipation of a full display of all its glory and beauty. As God reveals more and more of his redemptive plan, new revelation is always inseparably tied to his previous covenants. In fact, each successive covenant is but a renewal and an expansion of the previous covenants.

God's past dealings with his people provide the covenantal groundwork for a greater understanding of his purposes. God's covenants with Adam, Noah, Abraham, Moses, and David progressively expand the one covenant of grace. At each step in the developing revelation, God promises, "I shall be your God, and you shall be my people."[20] This theme resounds over and over until it reaches its climax in the person of Jesus Christ—"God with us" (Matt. 1:23).

The continuity of God's redemptive plan, from one administration of the covenant of grace to the next, is the predominant theme of the whole Bible. *This is covenant theology.* Any failure to grasp and appreciate the essential unity of God's purpose leads to confusion and misunderstanding. God's redemptive plan is both comprehensive—embracing every area of life—and unified in purpose.

What Does This Have to Do with Infant Baptism?

The inclusion of the children of believers in the covenant of grace is predicated on the continuity of the various covenantal administrations of that covenant of grace. God demonstrated, in each of the covenants, his redemptive concern for the individual believer, the believer's household, and the believer's society. This comprehensive redemptive plan extends to, and expands in, the new covenant, with all the blessings of the past and more. The new covenant will demonstrate a continuity with the past covenants and will be more inclusive than the previous covenantal administrations.

The households of believers in the Old Testament, including their infants, received the special privilege of God's redemptive covenants. These "little ones" of believers were marked out by God and set apart or sanctified from the rest of the fallen world. This inclusion of the children of believers in the covenant of grace was not a mere footnote in redemptive history. Rather, the children of God's people played a central role in God's redemptive plan from generation to generation. They continue to do so.

God commanded that even the infants of believers were to receive the covenant sign (circumcision) and be numbered among God's covenant people (i.e., the church). Baptism will have this same function as the new covenant unfolds the final redemptive revelation of the covenant of grace. The children of believers have always been included in God's redemptive covenants. The children of believers who are faithful to God's covenant will know the individual blessing of personal salvation. Covenant breakers will be cut off and receive the curses of the covenant.

NOTES

1. O. Palmer Robertson, *The Christ of the Covenants* (Phillipsburg, N.J.: Presbyterian and Reformed, 1980), 28. This book develops in more detail the unity of the various historical covenants.
2. An administration functions in a governmental role, applying

the laws or terms of that which it serves—e.g., a constitution or a covenant.

3. The covenant of grace is implied before the time of Abraham. It is more formally established in Genesis 17.

4. John Calvin, *Institutes of the Christian Religion,* ed. John T. McNeill (Philadelphia: Westminster Press, 1960), 2:446.

5. Much of the difficulty in grasping the concept of the covenants seems to center on problems with the language used. Terms are sometimes used interchangeably by different authors. For example, "the covenant of redemption," the "covenant of grace," or "the promise" may all refer to God's one redemptive plan from eternity through its historical development. The terms "historic covenants," "covenantal administrations," or "covenants of promise" refer to the particular covenants that God made with Adam, Noah, Abraham, Moses, and David, and sometimes to the new covenant. These particular covenants are but the individual parts, or the unfolding, of the one "covenant of grace."

6. A. A. Hodge, *Evangelical Theology* (1890; reprint, Carlisle, Pa.: Banner of Truth, 1990), 173.

7. John Gill, *A Complete Body of Doctrinal and Practical Divinity* (1809; reprint, Paris, Ark.: Baptist Standard Bearer, 1989), 903. Gill pastored the Metropolitan Tabernacle before C. H. Spurgeon.

8. Peter A. Lillback, "Calvin's Covenantal Response to the Anabaptist View of Baptism," in *The Failure of the American Baptist Culture,* ed. James B. Jordan, Christianity and Civilization, no. 1 (Tyler, Tex.: Geneva Divinity School, 1982), 188.

9. The church is the institution of redemption that brings God's Word to bear on the individual, the family, and the society.

10. Robertson, *Christ of the Covenants,* 106.

11. 1 Peter 3:20–21 speaks of spirits "who once were disobedient, when the patience of God kept waiting in the days of Noah, during the construction of the ark, in which a few, that is, eight persons, were brought safely through the water. And corresponding to that, baptism now saves you—not the removal of dirt from the flesh, but an appeal to God for a good conscience—through the resurrection of Jesus Christ." The New Testament sees the ark, and the salvation of Noah and his household, as a type of baptism. This "baptism" was applied to Noah's entire household.

12. E.g., we see in the Noahic covenant the establishment of the death

penalty for the crime of murder (Gen. 9:5–6). This penalty serves to protect society from evildoers.

13. "The righteousness of faith" (Rom. 4:13) is another way of saying "justification by faith."

14. Roderick Campbell, *Israel and the New Covenant* (Philadelphia: Presbyterian and Reformed, 1954), 20.

15. Robertson, *Christ of the Covenants,* 29.

16. There is little difference in what the Judaizers did and what thousands of "professing Christians" have done, in seeking salvation by works. A "works righteousness" was never taught or intended in the Mosaic covenant, any more than it is under the new covenant. This is a perversion of God's truth. We must avoid the mistake of confusing the perversion of the Judaizers with the true faith of the Jews. Understanding this is essential to the proper interpretation of Galatians and many other New Testament passages.

17. Campbell, *Israel and the New Covenant,* 34–35.

18. E.g., 1 Kings 2:3; 1 Chron. 16:15–16; Ps. 105:6, 9, 42.

19. O. Palmer Robertson, in *Christ of the Covenants* (p. 38), comments on the genealogical aspect of God's covenants: "Clearly the reference to a 'thousand' generations intends to depict the concept of an eternal covenant. But just to out-literalize the literalist interpreter for the moment, some quick calculations may be made on the assumption that God's covenant promises extend to a 'thousand' generations. Figuring on the basis of a modest 20 years per generation, the covenant promises would extend to 20,000 years. Since Abraham lived only 4000 years ago, at least the next 16,000 years are 'covered' by the promises of the Abrahamic Covenant."

20. Cf. Gen. 17:7; Ex. 6:6–7; Lev. 11:45; Deut. 4:20; 29:13; 2 Kings 11:17; 2 Chron. 23:16; Ezek. 34:24; Zech. 2:11; 2 Cor. 6:16; Heb. 8:10.

CHAPTER 4

The Promise Fulfilled: The Flower of Redemption

IT WAS THE DAY Mark had been waiting for—the climax of all those years of school. Today he would receive his Ph.D. "Dr. Marcus S. Warner" certainly sounded great! Mark's family and friends were proud of him and thrilled about this day of honor.

Many people had contributed to Mark's academic journey. His parents had been faithful to instruct him and to provide him with the best possible education. The dedication of Mrs. Eaves at Trinity Elementary School laid the foundation for Mark's future accomplishments. Mr. Brumley, the principal and science teacher at Emmanuel High, took Mark under his wing, and it was there that Mark first realized his ability in the physical sciences and focused his attention in that direction. His undergraduate work at Georgia Tech gave Mark the necessary skills for the advanced research he would later do in graduate school.

Of all the many schools and graduations—elementary, junior high, high school (valedictorian), college (B.A. in chemistry, *magna cum laude*)—none compared with today's ceremonies and honors. Yet, in a vital way, all of Mark's previous education contributed to this climactic moment. His past training made this event possible, although none of it matched this moment in its glory and finality.

GOD'S ADMINISTRATIONS of the covenant of grace in the Old Testament—the covenants made with Adam, Noah, Abraham, Moses, and David—were redemptive schools that led to the final redemptive climax of the new covenant. While the new covenant surpasses them in glory, power, and finality, it nevertheless stands on the successive covenants of promise. Their unity causes them to be mutually dependent on one another. The flower bud of redemption that was swelling from the first promise of the gospel in Genesis 3:15 until the close of the Old Testament finally manifests itself in the glory of its full bloom in the new covenant.

Transition from the Old to the New

Old Testament prophets expected the coming new covenant. They spoke of this glorious day in the context of covenantal history. They did not view the new covenant as something divorced from God's past redemptive dealings with his people. In fact, it was the "Spirit of Christ within them" (1 Peter 1:10–11) who was predicting what was to come. This covenant unity was to be expected because God's covenant promises were everlasting in character: "My covenant I will not violate, nor will I alter the utterance of My lips" (Ps. 89:34; cf. also 1 Chron. 16:15–17).

The older covenants laid the foundation for the new covenant. Instead of sweeping the older covenants aside, the new covenant builds on them and fulfills their promises. The covenants found in the Old Testament continue to have abiding validity and significance in the New Testament. In Jeremiah's prophecy, "'Behold, days are coming,' declares the LORD, 'when I will make a new covenant with the house of Israel and with the house of Judah'" (Jer. 31:31), we see the relationship of the new covenant with earlier covenants.

Ezekiel connected the Abrahamic, Mosaic, and Davidic covenants with the new covenant when he said,

> And My servant David will be king over them [Davidic], and they will all have one shepherd; and they will walk in My ordinances, and keep My statutes, and observe them [Mosaic]. And they shall live on the land that I gave to Jacob My servant, in which your fathers lived [Abrahamic]; and they will live on it, they, and their sons, and their son's sons, forever; and David My servant shall be their prince forever [Davidic]. And I will make a covenant of peace with them; it will be an everlasting covenant with them [New]. And I will place them and multiply them, and will set My sanctuary in their midst forever. (Ezek. 37:24–26)

Similarly, in the New Testament we find new covenant continuity with preceding covenants. Romans 16:20 looks back to the Adamic covenant. Peter draws a parallel with the Noahic covenant in 1 Peter 3:5–7. The new covenant is founded on the Abrahamic in Romans 4:16. The validity of the Mosaic is revealed in Romans 3:31. Romans 15:12 sees the new covenant as based on the Davidic covenant. Basic unity and progressive development are demonstrated in all the divine covenants.[1]

The Hebrew word for "new," *hadash,* used in reference to the new covenant in Jeremiah 31:31, is not the word meaning "brand new"; rather, it means "renewed" or "fresh." The new covenant, like previous covenantal administrations, added to and expanded the redemptive revelation of God. It renewed the previous covenants, rather than replacing them.

The Old Testament looked forward to the new covenant as the culmination of God's covenant faithfulness. God's people could always depend on his promises to them, and to their children, and to their children's children—to all who were covenant keepers. The Old Testament was not a failed experiment that had to be replaced by a new plan that would work. All God's purposes are perfectly accomplished in his one plan of redemption.

The Gospels

In the Gospels of the New Testament, Christ and his covenant unite with the covenants of promise—"The book of the genealogy of Jesus Christ, the son of David, the son of Abraham" (Matt. 1:1; cf. Luke 1:27). These are the very first words of the New Testament. From the beginning, Jesus is identified with both Abraham and David (Luke 1:32–33, 69).[2] The promised seed of Abraham was the fulfillment of the prophecy of Isaiah, who, in covenantal language, said, "'The virgin shall be with child, and shall bear a Son, and they shall call His name Immanuel,' which translated means, 'God with us'" (Matt. 1:23).[3] Christ would "shepherd" God's "people Israel" (Matt. 2:6). As Mary rejoiced over her coming child, she recalled God's promise to all faithful generations (Luke 1:50), and the fulfillment of the promises to Abraham and the fathers (Luke 1:54–55). The father of John the Baptist, Zacharias, prophesied that the Savior had come "to show mercy toward our fathers, and to remember His holy covenant, the oath which He swore to Abraham our father" (Luke 1:72–73).

The coming of Jesus, the promised Redeemer, was what the Old Testament had been all about. He was the object of all the covenants. That which had been expected by the fathers was now a reality. *Instead of doing away with those previous covenants, the birth of Jesus Christ validated and confirmed them*— "For I say that Christ has become a servant to the circumcision on behalf of the truth of God to confirm the promises given to the fathers" (Rom. 15:8).

The advent of Christ was not the beginning of something brand new; rather, it was the culmination and climax of God's ancient plan to save his people. The Old Testament was not passing away—it was expanding. The everlasting covenants of the fathers were indeed everlasting, and the birth of the Redeemer proved that God never turns from his promises.

Jesus told the Jews, "Your father Abraham rejoiced to see My day," and, "Before Abraham was born, I am" (John 8:56, 58). In Matthew 5:17–18 Jesus makes it clear that he did not come to annul the law of Moses, but to fulfill it.[4] It was Jesus that Moses had spoken of (Luke 24:44; John 1:45), and Jesus identified himself with Moses on the Mount of Transfiguration (Matt. 17:3–4). The parable of the rich man and Lazarus shows that Moses and the prophets were sufficient (if believed) to keep one out of hades and to secure a place in the bosom of Abraham (Luke 16:19–31). The Great Commission (Matt. 28:16–20) is rooted in the promise made to Abraham that he and his seed would be a blessing to the nations. Acts 2 implements that promise. John 4:21–23 tells us that "salvation is from the Jews." Campbell explains,

> In these words Jesus is telling us not merely that Christianity is historically successive; He is telling us that Christianity is the fulfillment, the ripened fruit, the accomplishment of that which was present in principle, in promise, in symbolic form, and in prophetic type, in the Old Covenant system.[5]

Christ was the very object of the historic covenants. They provide the context in which the new covenant is revealed. We must read and interpret the New Testament in the light of how first-century Jews (and later Gentiles) would have received it. They were thoroughly familiar with God's covenantal dealings with them, and would have expected God to continue his redemptive dealing with individuals, families, and society.

The Remnant

Most Baptists and Reformed paedobaptists agree that the work of John the Baptist was to mark out, via baptism, the faithful

remnant of Israel to prepare a people for the coming Lord.
John called for the repentance of unfaithful Jews. This calling
of some of "the lost sheep of the house of Israel" back to covenant faithfulness (i.e., covenant renewal), accompanied by the
outward sign of covenant renewal, baptism, fulfilled God's
promise to separate the covenant faithful from the covenant
unfaithful before the coming of the Lord (see Mal. 4).

Were there only unfaithful Jews present during the days
of John's ministry, or were there also those who were already
faithful to the covenant, that is, true believers? If there were
faithful Jews present (and Mal. 4 and Rom. 11:5 suggest that
this was the case), then they had no need to heed John's call to
repentance. Yet, in order to be marked out as part of the faithful remnant, they also stood in need of receiving the sign of
covenant renewal, which was water baptism.

Both the nominal Jews and the faithful remnant would
already have circumcised their household members, but only
the faithful remnant would also have implemented their covenant obligations to instruct their households in the faith of
their father Abraham (cf. Gen. 18:19). The unfaithful Jew, who
stood in need of repentance, followed only the outward form
(circumcision of the flesh), without concern for the inward reality (circumcision of the heart).

Household covenant obligations between parents and
their children featured prominently in John's call to repentance. In the last verse of the Old Testament we are told, concerning the ministry of John the Baptist, "And he will restore
the hearts of the fathers to their children, and the hearts of the
children to their fathers, lest I come and smite the land with a
curse" (Mal. 4:6). The angel Gabriel repeated this prophecy
when he described what the work of John would be: "And it is
he who will go as a forerunner before Him in the spirit and
power of Elijah, to turn the hearts of the fathers back to the
children, and the disobedient to the attitude of the righteous;
so as to make ready a people prepared for the Lord" (Luke
1:17).

These two passages form a hinge between the Old and

New Testaments, based on the necessity of covenant faithfulness in households. Instead of doing away with the covenant household, John's ministry confirmed the faithful covenant household as essential in preparing the way for the Lord and avoiding God's curse. There is no question, since John's ministry precedes the coming of the kingdom (cf. Matt. 11:11–12), that those hearing John's message thought in terms of covenant households. Both the unfaithful Jew who repented of neglecting his responsibilities to his covenant household, and the faithful Jew who was already doing what God expected, were no doubt marked out by John's baptism of covenant renewal along with their entire households.

John the Baptist

God anointed an infant in the womb to be the forerunner of Christ's kingdom and the new covenant (Luke 1:15). Some argue that John's ministry interjected a radical new element into God's redemptive plan—shifting from the corporate, external, and physical emphasis of the older covenants to the individual, internal, and spiritual emphasis of the new covenant. Yet, a closer look at John's ministry reveals that, instead of calling people to a new redemptive reality, he called them back to the original demands that God had placed on his covenant people. His first objective was to mark out a faithful remnant of God's covenant people, and his second was to call on the unfaithful Jew to repent and be counted among the covenant faithful. Alfred Edersheim comments on this point,

> As already shown, the Baptism of John was in itself only a consecration to, and preparatory initiation for, the new Covenant of the Kingdom. *As applied to sinful men* it *was* indeed necessarily a "baptism of repentance;" but not as applied to the sinless Jesus. Had it primarily and always been a "baptism of repentance," He could not have submitted to it.[6]

John's ministry was to the people of Israel, many of whom had forgotten their true faith and exchanged it for mere externalism and a false reliance on their physical relationship to Abraham. But God never intended for Israel to rely on anything other than the true faith of their father Abraham—faith in a promised Redeemer. Therefore, God sent John forth with this express purpose: "He will turn back many of the sons of Israel to the Lord their God. And it is he who will go as a forerunner before Him in the spirit and power of Elijah, to turn the hearts of the fathers back to the children, and the disobedient to the attitude of the righteous; so as to make ready a people prepared for the Lord (Luke 1:16–17).

John called on the nominal Jews to repent of their sins and return to the faith of their fathers. His baptism was a sign of their renewal and cleansing.[7] Moreover, John was not remiss in warning the unrepentant Jews (who knew better to start with) that they could expect judgment (covenant curses) for their covenant unfaithfulness (Matt. 3:1–9; Luke 3:7–9).

When the Pharisees and Sadducees came to him for baptism, John warned them that their reliance on a physical relationship to Abraham was not sufficient and that, because of their unfaithfulness, they could expect to be cut off.

> Do not suppose that you can say to yourselves, "We have Abraham for our father"; for I say to you, that God is able from these stones to raise up children to Abraham. And the axe is already laid at the root of the trees; every tree therefore that does not bear good fruit is cut down and thrown into the fire. (Matt. 3:9–10)

The Lord was pruning the dead branches from the olive tree (Rom. 11:16–24) in preparation for the new covenant of Jesus Christ. Only those who were faithful to the covenant would enjoy the promises made to the fathers. One of God's promises to Abraham was that he would be God to his children.

The Apostles and Covenant Continuity

The apostles recognized that they were the "heirs of the promise" (Gal. 3:29). Therefore, they repeatedly made reference to God's previous covenants and the New Testament believer's relationship to them. On the day that the new covenant was inaugurated—Pentecost—the apostle Peter addressed the Jews who were assembled in Jerusalem and assured them that "the promise is for you and your children, and for all who are far off, as many as the Lord our God shall call to Himself" (Acts 2:39). This was the familiar formula of the Abrahamic covenant, in which the promise was made to the believer Abraham, to his children, and to the nations (Gen. 17:1–8).[8]

In his next sermon (Acts 3:12–26), Peter continued to develop the theme of the fulfillment of the past covenant promises. Similarly, the covenants of promise provided the foundation for Stephen's sermon before the Sanhedrin in Acts 7:2–8. Paul tells us that the gospel was preached "beforehand to Abraham" (Gal. 3:8), and he ties his preaching of the gospel to the promise of the past covenants: "And now I am standing trial for the hope of the promise made by God to our fathers; the promise to which our twelve tribes hope to attain, as they earnestly serve God night and day. And for this hope, O King, I am being accused by Jews" (Acts 26:6–7).

Romans 4 confirms that it is through faith, like that of Abraham, that believers are justified and thereby enter the same covenant and receive the same promises (including the ones to their children). Paul asserts the permanence and validity of the promises of the covenants in Galatians 4:23, 28: "But the son by the bondwoman was born according to the flesh, and the son by the free woman through the promise. . . . And you brethren, like Isaac, are children of promise." It is new covenant believers whom Paul declares to be the children of Abraham and the recipients of Abraham's blessing:

Therefore, be sure that it is those who are of faith
who are sons of Abraham. . . . So then those who are
of faith are blessed with Abraham, the believer. . . .
For you are all sons of God through faith in Christ
Jesus. . . . And if you belong to Christ, then you are
Abraham's offspring, heirs according to promise. (Gal.
3:7, 9, 26, 29)

In writing to the Ephesians, Paul says that the Gentiles
had been "excluded from the commonwealth of Israel, and
strangers to the covenants of promise," but that "now in Christ
Jesus you who formerly were far off have been brought near
by the blood of Christ" (Eph. 2:12–13). And James addresses
the church as "the twelve tribes who are dispersed abroad"
(James 1:1; cf. also 1 Peter 1:1).

God has always had one plan of redemption—the covenant of grace. Instead of dealing with people in a series of
abrupt starts and stops, whereby he changes his methods of
dealing with them, God smoothly unfolds a single plan of redemption. He makes his promises of redemption and fulfills
them, from start to finish, with an essential unity and continuity. Pierre Ch. Marcel summarizes the supremacy of the covenant of grace in this way: "The doctrine of the covenant is the
germ, the root, the pith of all revelation, and consequently of
all theology; it is the clue to the whole history of redemption.
Every other doctrine, no matter what it may be, is in some
manner connected with it."[9]

The apostles never shied away from their covenantal roots.
Instead, they enthusiastically laid claim to the promises made
to the fathers. The centrality, unity, and continuity of the covenants is the heart of apostolic teaching and undergirds their
understanding of the new covenant. While they do distance
themselves from the perversions of the Old Testament faith
(e.g., the demand for circumcision by the Judaizers, Gal. 5:8),
they wholeheartedly embrace the true faith of the fathers and
demand a like faith from all those who would lay claim to new
covenant blessings.

Christ Confirms the Historic Covenants

The Bible clearly identifies Christ with the covenants found in the Old Testament. In fact, the ministry of Christ cannot be properly understood apart from them. At the close of the Old Testament, and in anticipation of the coming new covenant, we find this prophecy of the coming Savior (Mal. 3:1): "'Behold, I am going to send My messenger, and he will clear the way before Me. And the Lord, whom you seek, will suddenly come to His temple; and the messenger of the covenant, in whom you delight, behold, He is coming,' says the LORD of hosts."

Christ is the "messenger of the covenant."[10] This is confirmed in Hebrews 9:15, where we are told that Christ is "the mediator of a new covenant." As such, he is "a servant to the circumcision on behalf of the truth of God to confirm the promises given the fathers" (Rom. 15:8). One promise that Christ came to confirm was God's promise to Abraham that he would "be God to you and to your descendants after you" (Gen. 17:7). *Either the children of believing parents are still in the same covenant with their parents or else Christ did not confirm all the promises made to the fathers.*

If the children of believers are embraced by the promises of the covenant, as certainly they are, then they must also be entitled to receive the initial sign of the covenant, which is baptism. This is affirmed by Peter in Acts 2:38–39. The right of believers' children to be included in the covenant is based on Christ's faithfulness as the messenger of the covenant and as the one who confirms the promises made to the fathers.

Christ was sent as the messenger to fulfill the covenant made with Abraham: "Now the promises were spoken to Abraham and to his seed. He does not say, 'And to seeds,' as referring to many, but rather to one, 'And to your seed,' that is, Christ" (Gal. 3:16; cf. Gen. 17:7). Christ came so that those who believe in him might be "blessed with Abraham, the believer," and that "the blessing of Abraham might come to the Gentiles, so that we might receive the promise of the Spirit through faith" (Gal. 3:9, 14).[11] The Puritan theologian John Owen summarizes the matter when he says,

> This covenant was, that God would be "a God unto Abraham and to his seed;" which God himself explains to be his infant seed, Gen. xvii. 12.—that is, the infant seed of every one of his posterity who should lay hold on and avouch that covenant as Abraham did, and not else. This the whole church did solemnly for themselves and their posterity; whereon the covenant was confirmed and sealed to them all, Exod. xxiv. 7, 8. And every one was bound to do the same in his own person; which if he did not, he was to be cut off from the congregation, whereby he forfeited all privileges unto himself and his seed.
>
> The covenant, therefore, was not granted in its administrations unto the carnal seed of Abraham as such, but unto his covenanted seed, those who entered into it and professedly stood to its terms.[12]

The Promise

The ideas of covenants and promises go hand in hand. Remember, a covenant is a conditional promise. Each covenant that God made with man promised certain blessings for covenant keepers and curses for covenant breakers. The apostles were constantly aware of the covenant promises made to the fathers and emphasized the new covenant believer's relationship to them. But just what is "the promise" of the covenants in Ephesians 2:12? The verse states, "Remember that you [the Gentiles] were at that time separate from Christ, excluded from the commonwealth of Israel, and strangers to the covenants of promise, having no hope and without God in the world."

This promise was well known to those to whom the apostles were primarily speaking. The Gentiles were "strangers" not only to this promise, but also to the commonwealth of Israel. It was this same promise of Christ, made to Abraham, for which the twelve tribes waited to be fulfilled (Acts 26:7). Scripture is clear that there has been and continues to be only one promise whereby men are saved. We must conclude that the gospel of Christ, in all its fullness, is the promise made to the fathers.[13] Peter alludes to this promise in Acts 2:39, when he says, "For the promise is for you and your children, and for all who are far off, as many as the Lord our God shall call to Himself."

How would Peter's audience have understood that statement? It is important to keep the context of Peter's address in mind. Jews and Jewish proselytes had assembled in Jerusalem to celebrate Pentecost. Those he addressed were Parthians, Medes, Elamites, and other foreign Jews. It was about seven years later, at the house of Cornelius, before the first Gentiles were baptized. So, what did these Jews understand the promise to be? Their minds would immediately have recalled the Lord's great promise that he would be a God to Abraham and to his seed after him (Gen. 17:5). This was a promise that they would have heard of and talked about many times. Since they were now entering the new covenant era of the church, the question of their children's relationship to the church would naturally have been on their minds. Being a Jew, Peter was certainly aware of their concern and immediately moved to address the issue. He assured them that the promise was still for them and their children; because of this, he urged them to repent and be baptized. It is very difficult to explain Peter's language if he intended to exclude infant children.

Peter spoke to Jews who had a particular view of the household and the parent-child relationship. This view came from the Old Testament, and Peter indicated that it continued into the era of the new covenant. Modern Western culture may not share this view, but it is thoroughly biblical.

The promise of which Peter spoke was a promise made to Abraham in Genesis 17 (cf. Gal. 3:29). The promises of covenant blessing were initially made to three groups. First, the covenant was established between God and Abraham: "And I will establish My covenant between Me and you, and I will multiply you exceedingly" (Gen. 17:2).

Second, God extended his covenant to include descendants of the believer Abraham.

> And I will establish My covenant between Me and you and your descendants after you throughout their generations for an everlasting covenant, to be God to you and to your descendants after you. . . . God said further to Abraham, "Now as for you, you shall keep My covenant, you and your descendants after you throughout their generations." (vv. 7, 9)

Third, from the beginning the covenant had in view a multitude of nations.

> As for Me, behold, My covenant is with you, and you shall be the father of a multitude of nations. No longer shall your name be called Abram, but your name shall be Abraham; for I will make you the father of a multitude of nations. And I will make you exceedingly fruitful, and I will make nations of you, and kings shall come forth from you. (vv. 4–6)

There is an unmistakable similarity between the promise of the covenant in Genesis 17, as made with Abraham, his seed, and a multitude of nations, and the promise that Peter refers to in Acts 2:39. Peter tells his audience of Jews, "The promise is for you and your children, and for all who are far off, as many as the Lord our God shall call to Himself." He affirms to those now coming under the new covenant that God's eternal promise to Abraham is still valid for all who were initially embraced by it—believers, their children, and many nations.

Not every individual among these people would realize personal redemption—only those whom God called. Ishmael, Esau, and Judas were among these people, and they received the covenant sign and seal of circumcision; however, they were not called by God. Only those who were actually called would ever enjoy the full benefits of the covenant.[14]

The new covenant believer is a participant in the Abrahamic covenant as much as Abraham was. Believers and their children from both the old and the new era are partakers of the same covenant and its promises.[15] Those who argue for the end of the Abrahamic covenant because of the establishment of the new covenant run into a problem. Robert L. Dabney expressed their dilemma in this way: "How could the Abrahamic Covenant have expired before the Gentiles were brought into it? If it did expire prior to this event, then the promise was unfulfilled."[16]

Because of "the promise," Christ came and made us "heirs of the promise." As the children's Sunday school song teaches,

Father Abraham had many sons,
And many sons had father Abraham.
And I am one of them,
And so are you.
So, let's just praise the Lord.

The Abrahamic covenant was never intended to be temporary. It is the very foundation of God's redemptive plan. One prominent feature of the Abrahamic covenant is that it is "an everlasting covenant" (Gen. 17:7, 13; also, Luke 1:55). Since God is faithful to his Word, an everlasting covenant can never be revoked or replaced. Hence, the new covenant, instead of replacing the Abrahamic covenant, is the perpetual fulfillment of that covenant. The New Testament simply brings the covenant of grace to full bloom.[17] The Abrahamic covenant and its promises continue today. New Testament believers and their children are the recipients of its promised blessings and benefits (Gal. 3:29), as well as its threats of covenant curses (Rev. 2:5).

How Then Is the New Covenant New?

While continuity between the old covenants and the new covenant is both assumed and evident, this is not to say that the new covenant does not make some significant changes. What is it that makes the new covenant "new"? How is it better?

First, the new covenant brings with it, through the work of the Holy Spirit, and as a fulfilled promise of the Abrahamic covenant (Gal. 3:14), the enabling power of obedience (Jer. 31:33; Ezek. 11:20; Heb. 7:19). This enabling power of obedience is one of the better promises of the new covenant spoken of in Hebrews 8:6–8.[18]

Second, the new covenant promises an extension of the knowledge of the Lord to all nations (Heb. 8:11; Jer. 31:34; Matt. 28:19). All the world is to be taught about God's gracious covenant. More people are to know more about the Lord.

Third, the new covenant brings with it the promise of redemption accomplished. Under the older covenants, there was a continual reminder of sins (Heb. 10:3), but our high priest, Christ, has made a sacrifice for sins "once for all" (Heb. 7:27). The new covenant believer looks back on the completed work of Christ.

Finally, the new covenant is the final manifestation of God's redemptive plan. It is the full bloom of the flower of redemption, and it will not be exceeded in power, knowledge, or glory. There are no more covenant administrations to be revealed.

God's promise to Abraham was renewed or confirmed in the Mosaic administration of the promise. In the Mosaic covenant, God provided ceremonies as a perpetual reminder and instructor (i.e., tutor; cf. Gal. 3:24) of his promise of redemption made originally to Abraham. The new covenant is the fulfillment of God's original promise; the reminders and instructions have accomplished their purpose, have faded away, have become "obsolete" (Heb. 8:13), and are no longer necessary. The ceremonial aspects of the old covenant (e.g., the Levitical priesthood, the tabernacle and temple, and the animal sacrifices) have become obsolete, because their fulfillment in the person and work of Jesus Christ has left them with no further purpose. These ceremonial laws are still valid, but they have now been written on the hearts of believers (Heb. 8:10), and they find their fulfillment in Christ.[19]

To illustrate this point, imagine you owed someone a billion dollars. There is no way you could ever pay such a debt. Your creditor, instead of having you put in prison, mercifully has you sign an agreement that requires you to pay him one hundred dollars per month as a token of your debt to him. You both know that at that rate you will never come close to paying off your debt. The monthly payment simply acknowledges that you are a debtor. But suppose a very wealthy uncle paid the debt for you in full. Are you now still required to send the former creditor one hundred dollars per month? Of course not. You are no longer a debtor and the token payments no longer apply to your situation. In fact, to continue to make such token payments after your uncle paid your debt would show a lack of understanding of what he did.[20]

The new covenant administration of the covenant of grace is new in the sense that it expands the covenant of grace. It broadens its extent and application; it offers substance over shadow; it brings greater blessings—yet, it leaves intact the fundamental elements of the original covenant of grace. Robert L. Dabney saw the implications of this for the children of believers when he wrote,

> We understand that the new dispensation is an extension of the old one, more liberal in its provisions, and its grace: and embracing the whole human family. It would be a strange thing indeed, if this era of new liberality and breadth were the occasion for a new and vast restriction, excluding a large class of the human family, in whom the pious heart is most tenderly interested.[21]

The more narrow old administrations included the children of believers in the covenant of grace. They should therefore be included under the new and broader administration of the covenant of grace, barring an explicit statement by God to the contrary. As Dabney points out, "When a society undergoes important modifications, its substantial identity yet remaining, the fair presumption is, that all those things are intended to remain unchanged, about the change of which nothing is said."[22]

What Does This Have to Do with Infant Baptism?

The doctrine of infant (or household) baptism is built on the unity of the covenant of grace and its various administrations. As whole-Bible Christians, we must understand God's revelation in the context of his previous redemptive revelation. Failure to do so leads to a fractured, dispensational, and disunified view of God and Scripture. God made promises to Abraham, which included his children and his children's children. New covenant believers are the children of Abraham and therefore receive all the promises that God gave to him, including those made to our children and our children's children. Those promises have never been abrogated or modified by God, and we must therefore assume that he still desires to embrace them in his covenant of grace.

This does not automatically make infants believers; neither are they to be presumed regenerate. The children of believers, like their parents, must embrace the covenant in faithfulness to its duties of repentance and faith. Then, like the children of the old covenant, and only then, may they personally lay claim to the redemptive blessing of the covenant. Professor John Murray wrote,

> The argument in support of infant baptism is based upon the essential unity and continuity of the covenant of grace administered to Abraham, unfolded in the Mosaic and Davidic covenants, and attaining to its highest fruition in the new covenant. The new covenant is the administration of grace that brings to fulfilment the promise given to Abraham: "In thy seed shall all the nations of the earth be blessed" (Gen. 22:18). It is the blessing of Abraham that comes on the Gentiles through

Christ (Gal. 3:14). Abraham is the father of all believers, and they are Abraham's seed and heirs according to promise (Rom. 4:16–18; Gal. 3:7–9). The promises fulfilled in Christ were given to Abraham with covenantal confirmation. So it is proper and necessary to say that the new covenant is the fulfilment and unfolding of the Abrahamic covenant (cf. Gal. 3:15–17). . . .

. . . Since the infant seed of the faithful were embraced in the covenant relation, and there is no indication that this feature of covenant administration has been abrogated under the new covenant, the conclusion derived from the unity and continuity of covenant grace is that the same privilege belongs to the infant seed of believers under the new covenant.[23]

These implications of the continuity of the covenants from the Old to the New Testament can only be avoided by devising a theology that radically divorces itself from God's past redemptive covenants and establish the new covenant on its own grounds. Only by removing the Old Testament data from theological consideration may the children of believers be denied their historical right to a place in the covenant of grace. John Calvin saw these implications and wrote,

Indeed, it is most evident that the covenant which the Lord once made with Abraham (cf. Gen. 17:14) is no less in force today for Christians than it was of old for the Jewish people, and that this word relates no less to Christians than it related to the Jews. Unless perhaps we think that Christ by his coming lessened or curtailed the grace of the Father. . . . Accordingly, the children of the Jews also, because they had been made heirs of his covenant and distinguished from the children of the impious, were called holy seed (Ezra 9:2; Isa. 6:13). For this same reason, the children of Christians are considered holy; and even though born with only one believing parent, by the apostle's testimony they differ from the unclean seed of idolaters (1 Cor. 7:14). Now seeing that the Lord, immediately after making the covenant with Abraham, commanded it to be sealed in infants by an outward sacrament (Gen. 17:12), what excuse will Christians give for not testifying and sealing it in their children today?[24]

The testimony of both the Old and the New Testament is overwhelming when it comes to the theme of covenant unity. From the eternal redemptive purpose of the Trinity, via the covenants with Adam, Noah, Abraham, Moses, and David, to the climax of the glorious new covenant of Jesus Christ, God has had this as his purpose: "I will be your God, and you shall be my people." He has always purposed to redeem individuals (believers), their families (including their little ones), and their societies ("those who are far off"). He promised to do this in the Old Testament and he is fulfilling that promise in the age of the new covenant.

NOTES

1. Kenneth L. Gentry, Jr., *He Shall Have Dominion* (Tyler, Tex.: Institute for Christian Economics, 1992), 113–14.
2. Cf. also Matt. 21:9, 15; 22:42; Mark 10:47–48; Luke 18:38–39.
3. I call this language ("God with us") "covenantal" because it reflects the theme of all of God's redemptive covenants with man— "I will be your God, and you shall be my people." God's presence with his people is at the very heart of his covenantal relationship with them.
4. Throughout the New Testament there are appeals to the law of Moses [the Mosaic covenant], suggesting its continued validity. Here are but a few examples: Matt. 5:21, 27, 31, 38, 43; 19:7, 8; Mark 10:3, 4; 12:19, 26; Luke 16:29, 31; 20:28, 37; 24:27, 44. Cf. also Greg L. Bahnsen's books: *Theonomy in Christian Ethics*, 2d ed. (Phillipsburg, N.J.: Presbyterian and Reformed, 1984), and *By This Standard* (Tyler, Tex.: Institute for Christian Economics, 1985).
5. Roderick Campbell, *Israel and the New Covenant* (Philadelphia: Presbyterian and Reformed, 1954), 14.

6. Alfred Edersheim, *The Life and Times of Jesus the Messiah* (1886; reprint, McLean, Vir.: MacDonald, 19XX), 1:279–80.

7. John's baptism was not Christian baptism, although it was related to it—e.g., it was not Trinitarian and it applied to Jesus. The Jews were already familiar with various baptisms, or washings (cf. Heb. 9:10), so baptism would not have been new to them.

8. Because Acts 2:38 speaks of the "gift of the Holy Spirit," some have argued that it was solely the Holy Spirit that Peter was referring to as "the promise." However, Gal. 3:14 ties the blessing of Abraham to the promise of the Holy Spirit, "in order that in Christ Jesus the blessing of Abraham might come to the Gentiles, so that we might receive the promise of the Spirit through faith." In other words, the promise to Abraham was fulfilled in the gospel and the pouring out of the Holy Spirit in the new covenant.

9. Pierre Ch. Marcel, *The Biblical Doctrine of Infant Baptism,* trans. Philip Edgcumbe Hughes (1953; reprint, Cambridge: James Clark, 1981), 71.

10. The first "messenger" in this text, who "will clear the way," is John the Baptist. However, the "messenger of the covenant" is Christ. See T. V. Moore, *Zechariah, Haggai and Malachi*, Geneva Series of Commentaries (Carlisle, Pa.: Banner of Truth, 1974), 149; cf. John Calvin, *Calvin's Commentaries* (Grand Rapids: Baker, 1979), 15:569.

11. See John Owen, *The Works of John Owen* (Carlisle, Pa.: Banner of Truth, 1981), 16:261–62.

12. Ibid., 262.

13. Marcel, *Biblical Doctrine of Infant Baptism,* 77–78.

14. The notion that the phrase "as many as the Lord our God shall call to Himself" (Acts 2:39) is a new concept introduced to the new covenant by Peter cannot be maintained. The effectual calling of God was as necessary for Old Testament believers as it is for New Testament believers (e.g., Ishmael, Jacob, and Esau). Rom. 11:5 tells us that a faithful remnant of Israel, which remained in the first century, was a matter of "God's gracious choice." Being born into a covenant household and receiving the covenant sign and seal of circumcision never meant that the individual automatically received the covenant blessing of personal salvation. Every individual's redemption has always been contingent upon the effectual calling of God and the resultant covenant faithfulness of the one who was called.

70 The Promise Fulfilled:

15. Allen C. Guelzo, *Who Should Be Baptized? A Case for the Baptism of Infants* (Philadelphia: Reformed Episcopal Publication Society, 1985), 7–8, 11.
16. Robert L. Dabney, *Lectures in Systematic Theology* (1878; reprint, Grand Rapids: Zondervan, 1975), 782–83.
17. Cf. Luke 1:54–55, 68, 72–73; John 8:56–58; Acts 3:24–26; Rom. 4:16–18, 22–24.
18. The new covenant offers "better promises" in that it provides the realization of the old covenant shadows (Heb. 8:5).
19. The moral law was already written on the hearts of both believers (Deut. 6:6; 11:18; 30:14) and unbelievers (Rom. 1:19, 32; 2:14–15). The ceremonial laws have had a change of application. For example, Christ is now our Priest (Heb. 7:17, 26–28), our sacrifice (Heb. 7:27), and our tabernacle or temple (Rev. 21:3). Likewise, the believer himself is a priest (1 Peter 2:9), a sacrifice (Rom. 12:1), and a temple (1 Cor. 3:16). I am indebted to Sean Mahaffy for his study and insight on this issue, especially as it applies to Heb. 7–10.
20. This explains the problem discussed in Heb. 10:26–27.
21. Dabney, *Lectures in Systematic Theology*, 786.
22. Ibid., 785–86.
23. John Murray, *Collected Writings of John Murray*, (Carlisle, Pa.: Banner of Truth, 1977), 2:374.
24. John Calvin, *Institutes of the Christian Religion*, ed. John T. McNeill (Philadelphia: Westminster Press, 1960), 2:1329.

CHAPTER 5

Pruning and Grafting: God's People of the Old and New Covenants

BRIAN AND KATHY KNIGHT were exhausted. For several weeks before their son's wedding, they had been busy with showers, rentals, rehearsals, and similar events. Finally, it was all over. Their son Tom was now married to Linda, a lovely Christian lady whom Brian and Kathy adored. The young couple were headed off on their honeymoon and had committed themselves to establishing a new Christian household. Tom was entering a whole new phase of life.

BRIAN: Honey, our little boy is all grown up. It's hard to believe he's married and off on his own.

KATHY: It doesn't seem like any time since we were changing his diapers. When he was little, it was hard to imagine he would ever be an adult. When kids come into the world, they're so helpless; you have to teach them everything.

BRIAN: Yeah, I can remember looking forward to the day

when Tom would be old enough to mow the yard and dread-
ing the time when he would be old enough to drive.

KATHY: Well, I think all that instruction has paid off now.
He's a fine young man, and he and Linda will do just great!
They're going to make good parents, and I'm ready to be a
grandmother.

BRIAN: Come on Granny, let's go out to eat. Raising kids
is hard work and we need to celebrate.

GOD TOOK HIS PEOPLE in the Old Testament and nurtured them
like little children. He provided for all their needs—physical,
mental, and spiritual. He protected them from harm, instructed
them in the truth, disciplined them when necessary, and
brought them to a place of maturity.

Each of God's covenants represented a new phase in the
developing maturity of God's covenant people. Finally, the
church reached adulthood in the new covenant of Jesus Christ,
the goal of all God's rearing. He strove with them for a long
time, bringing them from infancy to maturity. In the new covenant his purpose, which he had from the beginning, was accomplished.

One People or Two Peoples of God?

Many Christians see a sharp division between the Old and New
Testaments. This is especially true when it comes to defining
God's people. They see the Old Testament people of God primarily as an ethnic group (the physical descendants of Abraham) and the focus of God's relationship to them as corporate,
external, material, and earthly.

When we come to the New Testament, these Christians
see a major shift taking place, and ethnic Israel is replaced by
spiritual Israel, which is the church. They argue that the church
was instituted in the New Testament and signals a change in
God's dealings with his people. The focus is now primarily on
individual, internal, and spiritual concerns. Instead of there
being one church, transcending both Old and New Testaments,

this dispensational and baptistic interpretation sees two different peoples of God—the Jews and the church. This artificial dichotomy, if consistently held, turns God's people of the Old Testament, as well as the Old Testament itself, into little more than a historical reference.

The Reformed and covenantal understanding of God's dealings with his people throughout the ages, instead of cutting God's child (i.e., his church) into two separate pieces, recognizes that God has had one people throughout all the ages. Although this one church has developed through various stages, she is still the same church from age to age. God has always made the same spiritual demands on his people— justification by faith alone, wholehearted devotion to him, and true spiritual worship. Nothing less has ever been acceptable. In all ages God has demonstrated his redemptive concern for individuals and their corporate relationships with the family, the church, and society.

God determines the terms of membership for his church.[1] In the Old Testament he included believers and the children of believers in the membership of his church; he has nowhere changed the terms of church membership. *Since God has not changed the terms of church membership, new covenant believers and their children are likewise included in his church.* To argue against including the children of believers in the church now is also to argue against including them in the older covenant administrations. God not only permits the children of believers to be in his church, but he also demands that they be counted among his people. Who then shall deny what God has required?

The Bible teaches that the people of God in the Old Testament and the people of God in the New Testament are one and the same people. Both Old and New Testament believers are saved by grace through faith in the Savior, and such faith is counted unto them as righteousness. Only those who share the faith of Abraham ("the father of all who believe," Rom. 4:11), in either Old or New Testament times, ultimately receive all the redemptive benefits of the Abrahamic covenant. God's people (i.e., the church) have always been spiritual in nature.

The new covenant people of God are an extension or expansion of the old covenant people of God. There is a progressive development of the church from the Old Testament to the New; however, there are not two separate peoples of God. There is only one covenant of grace throughout all the ages for all the people of God and their children. Since the Old Testament church was spiritual and included the children of believers, we must assume that the spiritual church of the New Testament also includes the children of believers.

The Spiritual Nature of God's Old Testament People

According to the dispensational or baptistic view, the Jews are the carnal people of God, who were part of a covenant concerned with external and corporate matters. By contrast, the new covenant people of God are the spiritual people of God. The new covenant is concerned with inward and individualistic matters and, at best, gives diminished attention to the external and corporate realities of redemption. This view emphasizes the differences between the old and new covenants, providing justification for treating the children of believers differently in each age. Calvin said of this view,

> They depict the Jews to us as so carnal that they are more like beasts than men. A covenant with them would not go beyond the temporal life, and the promises given them would rest in present and physical benefits. If this doctrine should obtain, what would remain save that the Jewish nation was satiated for a time with God's benefits (as men fatten a herd of swine in a sty), only to perish in eternal destruction? For when we mention circumcision and the promises attached to it, they at once reply that circumcision was a literal sign and its promises were carnal.[2]

Moreover, this focusing on externals obscures the inward and spiritual aspects of the older covenants. This enables dispensationalists or Baptists to make the new covenant stand out by comparison.[3]

But the baptistic perception of the Old Testament people of God is simply incorrect. The old covenant continually drives home the importance of heartfelt devotion to God and the necessity of the inward and individual aspects of redemption. These are not incidental matters in the Old Testament; they are the very heart of the Old Testament record. Richard Flinn demonstrates the old covenant concern for spiritual and inward matters.

> Clearly the Old Covenant, however, was just as much concerned with inward realities of man's being. The Covenant called for man to walk before God and be blameless (Gen. 17:1; Dt. 18:13); man had to worship God in spirit and in truth (Ex. 20:1–11) so that he loved God with all his heart, soul, strength, and mind (Dt. 6:5; 10:12); he had to fear God, serving him in love (Dt. 10:12; 6:13); he had to seek for the Lord his God, searching for him with all his heart and soul (Dt. 4:29); his heart had to be circumcised so that he would love the Lord his God with all his heart and with all his soul (Dt. 30:6). Moreover, God gave his covenant law, not merely as an earthly reality serving as a typical foreshadowing of eternal life, but to teach men to love their neighbors as they loved themselves (Lev. 19:18), to do justice, to love mercy, and to walk humbly with their God (Micah 6:8). Thus the law was holy, just, and good, and therefore spiritual (Rom. 7:12, 14), provided it was used lawfully—that is, as God intended it to be used (I Tim. 1:8).[4]

The Bible knows of only one true seed of Abraham—the spiritual seed, the elect, the children of the promise. The carnal seed, though circumcised in the flesh, was always rejected by God and brought under his covenant judgment as covenant breakers. That is true in both the Old Testament and the New. Consider Romans 4:11–16.

And he [Abraham] received the sign of circumcision, a
seal of the righteousness of the faith which he had while
uncircumcised, that he might be the father of all who
believe without being circumcised, that righteousness
might be reckoned to them, and the father of circumcision to those who not only are of the circumcision, but
who also follow in the steps of the faith of our father
Abraham which he had while uncircumcised. For the
promise to Abraham or to his descendants [lit., "seed"]
that he would be heir of the world was not through the
Law, but through the righteousness of faith. For if those
who are of the Law are heirs, faith is made void and
the promise is nullified; for the Law brings about wrath,
but where there is no law, neither is there violation.
For this reason it is by faith, that it might be in accordance with grace, in order that the promise may be
certain to all the descendants [lit., "seed"], not only to
those who are of the Law, but also to those who are of
the faith of Abraham, who is the father of us all.

Several important points in this passage prove that not
the Jews as such, but only believers are the true seed of
Abraham in both the Old and New Testaments. First, Abraham is pictured as the father of all who believe, both those
who are of the circumcision (the Jews) and those who are not
of the circumcision (all other nations). Second, the text emphasizes that not all those who are circumcised in the flesh
are the true seed (descendants) of Abraham, but only those
among them who believe.[5] Finally, these descendants alone
are promised that they would all be heirs of their father
Abraham. This passage speaks of one father Abraham, one
seed of Abraham, one promise given to that seed, and only
one way to obtain that promise, the way of righteousness,
which is by faith.[6]

God condemned people throughout the Old Testament for
empty ritualism and externalism and consistently demanded
heartfelt devotion and service (Pss. 34:15–18; 51:10–19). It has

never been acceptable to God for one to be an "outward Jew" only. Consider Romans 2:28–29: "For he is not a Jew who is one outwardly; neither is circumcision that which is outward in the flesh. But he is a Jew who is one inwardly; and circumcision is that which is of the heart, by the Spirit, not by the letter; and his praise is not from men, but from God." The only true Israelite was the person who had genuine faith in his heart, of which circumcision was a sign. Only believers have ever been the true seed of Abraham.[7]

The apostle Paul was not introducing something new when he argued in this way. This had always been the requirement of God. The physical Jew was never to place any confidence in the flesh. That always stood in direct contradiction to what God expected from his people.

Spiritual descent has to do with faith, not DNA. Anyone who received the covenant sign of circumcision, whether as an adult or an infant, but who did not embrace and own that covenant by faith, was never a true heir of Abraham and did not obtain the promised blessing, which is redemption.[8] God's people have always and only been saved by grace through faith in Jesus Christ. God's people have always been united in the one seed of Abraham, which is Christ. The Old Testament believer had much more knowledge of saving truth than most people think (see John 8:56; Gal. 3:8; 2 Peter 2:5; Jude 14–15). How can we think that New Testament believers have greater faith than the "father of faith," Abraham, or more than Moses or Joshua?[9]

From the beginning, the spiritual aspects of the promise were primary. The physical aspects were but signs, types, and shadows that pointed to the spiritual realities. These spiritual realities were present from the beginning, but they became more and more apparent throughout redemptive history, culminating in the revelation of the new covenant.

The material blessings were never devoid of their spiritual meaning, even in the Old Testament. The promised seed of Abraham was always Christ (Gal. 3:16), yet Isaac was the type. The gospel was always the blessing that was intended for the many nations (Gal. 3:8), typified in the expanding nation of Israel. Heaven was always the promised land that Abraham looked for (Heb. 11:13–16), typified by the land of Canaan. Justification by faith was always the spiritual necessity (Rom. 4:10–11), typified by circumcision (and later by baptism). The physical sign of the promise may change or completely disappear, yet the spiritual reality continues from the beginning; it is not an added feature of the new covenant.

Perverting the Original Intent

The covenant of grace, as set forth in the Old Testament, was not always understood. It was perverted into the false idea of a salvation based on works or physical descent. The Pharisees and Judaizers turned the covenant of grace into a covenant of works, and they were rebuked for it by Jesus and the apostles (see Rom. 4:13; Gal. 3).

Misunderstanding of the way of salvation taught in the Old Testament has led many to believe that the New Testament opposes the Old Testament. Pitting the New against the Old, some have even supposed that there is a "God of the Old Testament" who stands over against the "God of the New Testament." Some imagine themselves to be "New Testament Christians" as opposed to "whole-Bible Christians." The result has been a disjointed and discontinuous view of the Bible, void of a unified message.

Only the Reformed and covenantal view of Scripture does justice to God's redemptive revelation. The Old Testament never calls for sinners to be justified by keeping the law. Justification has always been by faith alone, in the Old Testament no less than in the New. The New Testament simply argues against the *perversion* of the everlasting covenant of grace, not against the old covenant itself. Biological descent from Abraham was never a sufficient reason for one to expect covenant blessings. The only ones ever to receive these spiritual blessings were those who were faithful to the covenant themselves, as Calvin noted.

Intending to show the Jews how God's goodness was
not bound to the offspring of Abraham, indeed that of
itself such descent conferred nothing, Paul cites, by way
of proof, Ishmael and Esau [Rom. 9:6–13], who were
rejected just as if they were strangers; even though they
were real offspring of Abraham according to the flesh,
the blessing rests upon Isaac and Jacob. From this follows what he afterward affirms, that salvation depends
upon God's mercy, which he extends to whom he pleases
[Rom. 9:15–16]; but that there is no reason for the Jews
to preen themselves and boast in the name of the covenant unless they keep the law of the covenant, that is,
obey the Word.[10]

The entire fourth chapter of Romans is devoted to arguing that the only way anyone has ever been justified before
God, in both the Old and New Testament eras, is by faith in
the promise (i.e., the gospel) of God alone. Abraham was not
justified by works (v. 2), but by faith (v. 3). The faith of Abraham preceded his circumcision (v. 10), which was given as a
covenant sign and seal of righteousness by faith (v. 11). As a
result, the promise given to Abraham, appropriated by faith,
is also for his descendants, not through works, but by faith (v.
13). Works righteousness (i.e., keeping the law) could never
save; indeed, it would nullify the promise of redemption by
grace (vv. 14–15). It has always been by faith alone that one
has become an heir to the promise of redemption and that
one has thereby become a descendant of Abraham (vv. 16–17).
We are told that Abraham's faith was recorded not just for his
sake, but also for our sake, who also believe in God and his
gracious work of redemption (vv. 23–25).

The promise of redemption by grace is the central feature of the covenant of grace, permeating the whole Bible. As
the Westminster Confession of Faith states in the last para-
graph of chapter 11, "The justification of believers under the
Old Testament was, in all these respects, one and the same
with the justification of believers under the New Testament."[11]

If justification by grace through faith in the promised Redeemer has indeed always been God's only method of saving sinners, and if this plan of redemption has always been the key feature of the covenant of grace, we are left to consider the covenantal status of the children of believers. Abraham believed the promise of God, and God counted it as righteousness, giving him the sign and seal of circumcision as an indication of his covenant relationship with him. *God also required Abraham to give that same sign and seal to all who came under his household authority, including his children.* These children could only be justified by faith alone, yet they certainly were not able to express such faith as infants. They were children of the covenant—children of the promise. Nevertheless, the covenant had not yet been owned by them, nor had the promise been appropriated by faith. This faith would be their covenant obligation—an obligation they received from their believing parents. The condition of the promise was faith. Without faith, circumcision would not bring a blessing. Instead, it brought God's judgment against them as covenant breakers.

Since children in the Old Testament were always included by the covenant of grace and obligated to manifest faith, we must assume their continued inclusion and obligation in the New Testament. Since the New Testament has not cut them off from this benefit and obligation, we may not presume to do so ourselves. Neither circumcision nor baptism saves an infant; rather, it points to God's covenant claim on them and the necessity of genuine faith to appropriate the promised redemption of the covenant of grace in Christ.

Individualism and the Corporate Concerns of the New Covenant

The dispensational and baptistic view that God has turned his attention primarily to individual believers does not do justice to the Scriptures. It fails to appreciate the spiritual and inward focus of the older covenants, as well as the external and corporate redemptive concerns of the new covenant.[12] Individualistic thinking has clouded the ability of many Christians to think covenantally and corporately. Christians living in twentieth-century America have been especially steeped in the idea of the rugged individual. Such a focus, coupled with the de-emphasis on the corporate elements of human life would have been foreign to the people of the Old and New Testaments. The New Testament must be read against the backdrop of Old Testament customs familiar to first-century Palestinians. We may not read our individualistic American culture back into the first century. Commenting on the individualistic assumptions of Baptists, Vern S. Poythress writes,

> Jews of Jesus' time, like some tribal societies today, had a high level of conviction of the cohesiveness of societal units like family, tribe, and nation. The incident in Joshua 7:24–25 involves Achan *and his family.* The incident in Numbers 16:27 involves Dathan and Abiram and their families. The family of Dathan stood in solidarity with him, even though judgment was threatening (16:26). Why didn't they obey Moses when it was evident from the word of the Lord in 16:20–23 that the cause of Korah was lost? It was utterly foolish. But it becomes sociologically more intelligible if people operated in terms of family solidarity.[13]

The redemptive intent of the blood of Christ extends beyond the important but narrow concerns of individual salvation. Like the older administrations of the covenant of grace, God's redemptive concerns in the new covenant extend to the corporate and physical aspects of man's life, for example, his family and his society. The new covenant, like the older covenants, addresses husbands, wives, children, slaves, households, the visible and local church, the state, crime, politics, economics, social ethics, labor, education, the nations, and even our eating and drinking. These are not peripheral matters that are simply footnotes to redemption; they are important concerns throughout the Bible. Moreover, as individuals are redeemed, every area of life is brought under the influence of redemption! The blood of Christ is powerful to redeem all things—"the summing up of all things in Christ, things in the heavens and things upon the earth" (Eph. 1:10). It was the Father's will "through Him to reconcile all things to Himself, having made peace through the blood of His cross; through Him, I say, whether things on earth or things in heaven" (Col. 1:20).

The baptistic perception that the new covenant does not have much concern for the redemption of the external and corporate aspects of man's life has led to an unbalanced and disproportionate emphasis on individualism and has fostered a situation in which the church is less and less influential in American culture. Only a covenantal view of redemptive history can do justice to the comprehensive concerns of the gospel.

The baptistic view of both history and the future is not supported by the Bible. Both the old and new covenants show concern for the redemption of both the internal and the external aspects of people. The new covenant offers a greater realization than the old did because redemption has been accomplished and applied with power and fullness—internally and externally. Since there can be no objection to circumcising children under the old covenant, there is even less reason to object to baptizing children under the new. The new covenant redeems every aspect of creation.[14] The people of God— the church—in both the Old and New Testaments, are the same. God's redemptive concerns are likewise the same in both eras for individuals, households, and societies: both internal and external, physical and spiritual, and personal and corporate.

One Church

There is only one people of God, the church, established in the Old Testament and brought to maturity in the New Testament.[15] To make this point even more sure, let us compare some Old and New Testament passages. First, compare Hosea 1:10–11 with Romans 9:24–26. In Hosea we read,

> Yet the number of the sons of Israel will be like the sand of the sea, which cannot be measured or numbered; and it will come about that, in the place where it is said to them, "You are not My people," it will be said to them, "You are the sons of the living God." And the sons of Judah and the sons of Israel will be gathered together, and they will appoint for themselves one leader, and they will go up from the land, for great will be the day of Jezreel.

Paul does not hesitate at all in Romans 9 to apply this passage from Hosea to the church of the new covenant.[16] He says,

> Even us, whom He also called, not from among Jews only, but also from among Gentiles. As He says also in Hosea, "I will call those who were not My people, 'My people,' and her who was not beloved, 'Beloved.' And it shall be that in the place where it was said to them, 'You are not My people,' there they shall be called the sons of the living God."

Compare also Jeremiah 31:31–34 with Hebrews 8:6–13. In the first passage, Jeremiah speaks of a new covenant that the Lord will make with Israel and Judah.

> "Behold, days are coming," declares the LORD, "when I will make a new covenant with the house of Israel and with the house of Judah, not like the covenant which I made with their fathers in the day I took them by the hand to bring them out of the land of Egypt, My covenant which they broke, although I was a husband to them," declares the LORD. "But this is the covenant which I will make with the house of Israel after those days," declares the LORD, "I will put My law within them,

and on their heart I will write it; and I will be their
God, and they shall be My people. And they shall not
teach again, each man his neighbor and each man his
brother, saying, 'Know the LORD,' for they shall all know
Me, from the least of them to the greatest of them,"
declares the LORD, "for I will forgive their iniquity, and
their sin I will remember no more."

The Hebrews passage quotes this passage, which speaks
so plainly and specifically of Israel and Judah, and applies it to
the church of the new covenant.[17]

If there is not a unity of the church in the old and new
covenants, how can Christ claim that he has the keys of the
house of David (see Isa. 22:22; Rev. 3:7)?[18] The land of
Canaan, which was promised as an everlasting possession to
Abraham and his seed, is not only the earthly land near the
Mediterranean Sea, but also the heavenly land that is to
come, when the New Jerusalem shall come down. Such was
the hope of the old patriarchs, as is seen in Hebrews 11:8–
10, 13–16.

By faith Abraham, when he was called, obeyed by going out to a place which he was to receive for an inheritance; and he went out, not knowing where he was
going. By faith he lived as an alien in the land of promise, as in a foreign land, dwelling in tents with Isaac
and Jacob, fellow heirs of the same promise; for he was
looking for the city which has foundations, whose ar-
chitect and builder is God. . . . All these died in faith,
without receiving the promises, but having seen them
and having welcomed them from a distance, and having confessed that they were strangers and exiles on
the earth. For those who say such things make it clear
that they are seeking a country of their own. And indeed if they had been thinking of that country from
which they went out, they would have had opportunity
to return. But as it is, they desire a better country, that

is a heavenly one. Therefore God is not ashamed to be called their God; for He has prepared a city for them.

The whole Word of God teaches the unity of the people of God and all that pertains to them. All the promises are fulfilled in Christ, and through Him they are also for the true seed of Abraham in all ages, that is, believers.[19] "For as many as may be the promises of God, in Him they are yes; wherefore also by Him is our Amen to the glory of God through us" (2 Cor. 1:20). God does not function in a disjointed way. His redemptive plan is one of harmony, flowing smoothly through the ages to accomplish its purposes among his people, the church. A. A. Hodge answers the question, "What is the Church?" in this way:

> There is one thing certain about it: the Church has a great many attributes, but that which is absolutely essential is its absolute unity. There is no doubt if there be but one God, there is but one Church; if there be but one Christ, there is but one Church; if there be but one cross, there is but one Church; if there be but one Holy Ghost, there is but one Church. This is absolutely settled—there can be but one Church.[20]

The Olive Tree

God provides a vivid illustration of the unity of his people from one age to the other. In Romans 11:17–24 (cf. also John 15:1–11), he reveals that the Old Testament church continued under the new covenant. The good olive tree was not uprooted, but pruned, and new branches were grafted in.

> But if some of the branches were broken off, and you, being a wild olive, were grafted in among them and became partaker with them of the rich root of the olive tree, do not be arrogant toward the branches; but if you are arrogant, remember that it is not you who sup-

ports the root, but the root supports you. You will say
then, "Branches were broken off so that I might be
grafted in." Quite right, they were broken off for their
unbelief, but you stand by your faith. Do not be con-
ceited, but fear; for if God did not spare the natural
branches, neither will He spare you. Behold then
the kindness and severity of God; to those who fell,
severity, but to you, God's kindness, if you continue in
His kindness; otherwise you also will be cut off. And
they also, if they do not continue in their unbelief, will
be grafted in; for God is able to graft them in again.
For if you were cut off from what is by nature a wild
olive tree, and were grafted contrary to nature into a
cultivated olive tree, how much more shall these who
are the natural branches be grafted into their own
olive tree?

In that passage of Scripture, Paul uses the image of an
olive tree, one with a "rich root," to represent the church of
God. Many of the Jews, who were the natural branches, were
broken off because of their covenant unfaithfulness. The result was not the destruction of the olive tree. In fact, the tree
remained healthy and the Gentile branches of a wild olive tree
were grafted into it. This is a beautiful picture of the fact that
the New Testament church was a continuation of the Old Testament church.

Paul also looks forward to a time when the Jews, the natural branches, will be restored to the olive tree. They will be
grafted back into their own tree. In other words, they will be
reinstated in the very church from which they were cut off for
unbelief.[21] How could Paul be any more explicit about the essential unity of the church in both the Old and New Testaments? The Puritan John Flavel comments on this passage.

It is clear to me, beyond all contradiction, from Rom.
xi.17. "If some branches be broken off, and thou being
a wild olive-tree, wert grafted in amongst them, and

with them partakest of the root and fatness of the olive-tree:" I say I can scarce desire a clearer scripture-light than this text gives, to satisfy my understanding in this case, that when God brake off the unbelieving Jews from the church, both parents and children together, the believing Gentiles, which are as truly Abraham's seed as they were, Gal. iii.29, yea, the more excellent seed of Abraham, were implanted or ingrafted in their room, and do as amply enjoy the privileges of that covenant, both internal and external, for themselves and for their infant-seed, as ever any members of the Jewish church did or could.[22]

The same triune God was worshiped and obeyed in both the Old and the New Testament. Believers in both eras submitted to the same ethical standards found in the law and they received the same gospel; for "we have had good news preached to us, just as they also" (Heb. 4:2). Both groups of believers looked by faith to the same Savior, whose shed blood brought atonement for their sins. They taught the same fundamental truths, were saved on the same terms (i.e., faith and repentance), and required the same qualifications for church membership. What could be lacking to prove that the church of the patriarchs and prophets was the same in substance as it is in the New Testament era? Charles Hodge comprehended this truth and wrote,

> *The Commonwealth of Israel was the Church.* (1.) It is so called in Scripture. (Acts vii.38.) (2.) The Hebrews were called out from all the nations of the earth to be the peculiar people of God. They constituted his kingdom. (3.) To them were committed the oracles of God. They were Israelites; to them pertained the adoption, and the glory, and the covenants, and the giving of the law, and the service, and the promises. (Rom. ix.4.) Nothing more can be said of the Church under the new dispensation. They were selected for a Church purpose,

namely, to be witnesses for God in the world in behalf
of the true religion; to celebrate his worship; and to
observe his ordinances. Their religious officers, prophets, and priests, were appointed by God and were his
ministers. No man could become a member of the Commonwealth of Israel, who did not profess the true religion; promise obedience to the law of God as revealed
in his Word; and submit to the rite of circumcision as
the seal of the covenant. There is no authorized definition of the Church, which does not include the people
of God under the Mosaic law.[23]

The Nature of the Church

Baptists have maintained their well-intentioned belief in, and
desire for, a fully regenerate church membership. We all must
abhor a nominal church. Nevertheless, as admirable as this
desire may be, such an idyllic situation does not exist now, nor
do we see it in Scripture. The invisible church consists of the
spiritually faithful, who "abide" in Christ (John 15). Nevethe-
less, the members of the visible church are marked out by baptism and actual membership in a local church.[24] Regeneration
and faith are spiritual and invisible realities, and therefore, as
John Murray says, "No man or organization of men is able
infallibly to determine who are regenerate and who are not."[25]

   People have never been able (nor will they ever be able)
to determine with certainty the spiritual condition of someone's heart. If people can deceive themselves about their
own spiritual condition, then certainly they can deceive others, intentionally or unintentionally. The criteria that we are
given in Scripture for adult membership in the visible church,
whether in the Old Testament or the New, are such that
anyone, at least for a time, may meet them outwardly. Those
criteria are (1) basic comprehension of the Christian faith,
(2) a credible profession of faith,[26] and (3) an outward obedience to the Word of God.

   We have all known people who met these standards and

who either did not continue in them or else remained in the church while showing little or no signs of inward grace. In fact, if such a person never commits an excommunicable offense, he may die unregenerate and in full membership in the visible church.

The attempt to know people's hearts has led to many excesses in the search and demand for evidence of true conversion. As a Baptist minister, I was always troubled when called on to judge the genuineness of someone's "conversion experience." It was all so subjective on the part of the convert, as well as on the part of those who were evaluating the experience. Although we see the dramatic conversion of Saul and read that God "opened Lydia's heart," yet the ordinary accounts of salvation in the Bible are not especially dramatic. People repented, believed, and professed faith; these are the essential elements. God works in a diversity of ways with a diversity of people to accomplish his saving work. Some conversions are outwardly dramatic; others are outwardly more mundane and therefore impossible for men to discern.

Whether a conversion is ordinary or dramatic has no bearing on the genuineness of the miracle of regeneration. Men are still tempted, in their quest for the "regenerate church," to set up extrabiblical standards to test for genuineness; tears, turmoil, trembling, tongues, etc., are examples of the seal of approval. Others propose a waiting or testing period before allowing people into the visible church.[27] Such extrabiblical standards or proofs of regeneration have led many, who may be truly regenerate but have not experienced these particular "evidences," to question the genuineness of their conversion or to be unduly discouraged. On the other hand, some who have produced these "proofs" may have gained a false assurance of salvation. Along with these difficulties, I have seen ministers who came to believe that they could "discern," in some mystical fashion, whether someone was truly converted. We do not see such judgments being made in the Bible on the basis of such subjective or mystical criteria.

Another difficulty arising among some Baptists is that each

crisis of assurance leads to the question, "Do I need to be re-baptized?" Some have been rebaptized repeatedly in search of full assurance. I have personally experienced this problem, having been baptized twice. Feeling that one must match the particular salvation experiences of others can bring unwarranted vexation to young Christians, leading to unnecessary doubt. If, as Baptists declare, baptism is for believers only, then rebaptisms would be routine whenever there is any question of the genuineness of the original profession.

On the Reformed paedobaptist view, a baptized church member who has had a crisis of assurance would be counseled to abstain from the Lord's Supper until he has examined himself, to the end that he might partake (1 Cor. 11:28). Upon gaining assurance before God, the professing believer, instead of being rebaptized, would simply return to the Lord's Table to commune with him.

There is no question that among the members of the visible church some are indeed unregenerate and in need of being born again. That is true for both Baptists and Reformed paedobaptists. Even the Lord, who does infallibly know the hearts of men, allowed Judas to remain with him as an apostle. Certainly Judas had fooled the other disciples, for when Jesus said that one of them would betray him, they did not all immediately turn and point the finger at Judas. It was never God's expectation that the visible church would contain only regenerate people.

What Does This Have to Do with Infant Baptism?

Infants of believing households were clearly included in the church of the Old Testament, and in time they received all the benefits and incurred all the obligations of their membership. The male infants of believers received the covenant sign, which sealed their status as members of the covenant. This made them members of the visible church. God knew both their liabilities and their capabilities when he ordered their inclusion. Where is the warrant to bar the children of believers from this same church today? Ashbel Fairchild, writing more than a hundred years ago, pressed home that question.

> When and where has the God of heaven revoked the right? We call upon the advocates of "direct warrant" to answer the question. The burden of proof in this case rests upon them. Let them tell us when and where the Supreme Legislator has declared that infants, though once admitted into his church, are now forever excluded. Let them point us to even the least shadow of authority for thrusting little children out of the kingdom of heaven. They can produce none neither in the Old Testament or the New. In the absence of such authority, any attempt to deprive infants of the right of membership, is a virtual attempt to set aside the laws of God. It is more: it is undertaking to legislate in opposition to the authority of Jehovah! . . . We see, more clearly than ever, why the Saviour gave no express command, in so many words, to the disciples, to receive infants into the church. For, as he made no change in respect to membership, they perfectly understood that the same persons were to be admitted as formerly. The church being essentially the same under both dispensations, and baptism having been substituted for circumcision as the initiatory rite, it followed, as a matter of course, that infants still retained the right of membership, and consequently were to be baptized.[28]

Practically speaking, most Baptists recognize, and acknowledge by their language, that the "children of the church" are in a category separate from other children. They therefore teach their unbaptized children to pray and praise God. They often refer to households as "Christian families," even though several of the family's members may not have personally professed faith. These families are thought of as "Christian" because the head of the home is Christian. They recognize informally what God has said should be recognized formally—

that the children of believers hold a privileged status before
God, and that, while they may not have yet personally embraced the faith, they have been marked out by God as those
who are blessed to receive the benefits of the visible church.

There is but one church—one people of God—extending from the beginning to the end of time. Its membership
consists of believers and their households. Charles Hodge sums
it up well: "This is really the turning point in the controversy
concerning infant church-membership. If the Church is one
under both dispensations; if infants were members of the
Church under the theocracy, then they are members of the
Church now, unless the contrary can be proved."[29]

NOTES

1. The term *church* is used in several different ways. There is the
   universal church, which consists of God's elect in all times and in
   all places. Then there is the church visible and invisible, as viewed
   from human and divine perspectives. The visible church consists
   of all those who, at any given moment, are baptized members in
   good standing of local church bodies throughout the world. The
   invisible church is what God alone infallibly sees when he looks
   at the visible church and discerns those who are his elect, in addition to those who are already in heaven and not seen by us.
   The word *church* may also refer to a local assembly. I will be referring to the visible church unless otherwise noted.
2. John Calvin, *Institutes of the Christian Religion,* ed. John T. McNeill
   (Philadelphia: Westminster Press, 1960), 2:1333.
3. Richard P. Flinn, "Baptism, Redemptive History, and Eschatology: The Parameters of the Debate," in *The Failure of the American Baptist Culture,* ed. James B. Jordan, Christianity and
   Civilization, no. 1 (Tyler, Tex.: Geneva Divinity School, 1982), 136.
4. Ibid., 137.
5. Rev. 3:9 describes the false Jews as "those of the synagogue of
   Satan, who say that they are Jews, and are not, but lie." Like
   many who profess to be Christians, but are not (cf. Matt. 7:21–
   22), not all who claimed to be Jews were truly sons of Abraham
   (cf. Rom. 9:6–7). Only the covenant faithful had the required
   circumcision of the heart to be true Israelites (cf. Jer. 9:25).

6. Herman Hoeksema, *Triple Knowledge: An Exposition of the Heidelberg Catechism* (Grand Rapids: Reformed Free Publishing, 1971), 532.

7. Ibid., 532–34.

8. This is likewise true of baptism. Whether infant or adult, any baptism that is not coupled with a life of faith serves only to condemn its recipient.

9. Roderick Campbell, *Israel and the New Covenant* (Philadelphia: Presbyterian and Reformed, 1954), 32.

10. Calvin, *Institutes*, 2:1336.

11. Exactly the same statement is found in the 1689 London Baptist Confession of Faith.

12. The term *corporate* means "combined or unified into one body." Thus, when we speak of "corporate redemptive concerns," we have in view God's plan to redeem not only individuals separately, but also corporate units such as families or societies.

13. Correspondence from Vern S. Poythress, March 3, 1993.

14. Flinn, "Baptism, Redemptive History, and Eschatology," 151.

15. For an excellent study on this topic, see Charles D. Provan, *The Church Is Israel Now* (Vallecito, Calif.: Ross House, 1987). In this work, the author demonstrates how the Old Testament titles and attributes of Israel are applied to the Christian church in the New Testament. E.g., "the beloved of God," "the children of God," "the field of God," "the flock of God," "the house of God," "the kingdom of God," "the people of God," "the priests of God," "the vineyard of God," "the wife (or bride) of God," "the children of Abraham," "the chosen people," "the circumcised," "the olive tree." The people of God in both Testaments are called Israel; the new covenant is made with both Israel and the church.

16. See Hoeksema, *Triple Knowledge*, 535–36.

17. Ibid., 536. Compare also Amos 9:11–15 with Acts 15:13–17. The Amos passage seems to be nothing more than a prophecy of a literal restoration of Israel to their own land. Yet in Acts 15 we see James explain that this restoration of the tabernacle of David is now fulfilled in the new covenant as the Gentiles enter into fellowship with Christ.

18. Also, we could not explain why the Scriptures teach so plainly that Jerusalem and Mount Zion are not destroyed, but that they are now realized in the new covenant, while only the shadows are gone (cf. Isa. 28:16; Rom. 9:33; Gal. 4:25–26; 1 Peter 2:6;

Heb. 12:22; Rev. 21:2, 10). The same is true of the temple, the alter, the Holy Place, the sacrifice, and the high priest (cf. Heb. 9:1–12, 21–24; 10:19–21; 1 Cor. 3:16; 2 Cor. 6:16; Eph. 2:18–22; Rev. 3:12). All of God's provisions for his people in the Old Testament are continued in the New Testament, and his promises to them are fulfilled there.

19. Hoeksema, *Triple Knowledge*, 538–39.

20. A. A. Hodge, *Evangelical Theology* (1890; reprint, Carlisle, Pa.: Banner of Truth, 1990), 174.

21. This poses a problem for the individualistic interpretation of church membership. Are the individual branches that are cut off or grafted in only regenerate individuals? If so, how could they ever be cut off for unbelief? The pruning and grafting make sense only if we think in terms of peoples (e.g., Jews and Gentiles) and households, in which individuals may turn out to be covenant keepers or covenant breakers.

22. John Flavel, *The Works of John Flavel* (London: Banner of Truth, 1968), 3:545.

23. Charles Hodge, *Systematic Theology* (Grand Rapids: Eerdmans, 1981), 3:548–49.

24. We could say that the visible church also has an invisible aspect. The invisible church is infallibly seen by God, while the visible church is seen by fallible men.

25. John Murray, *Christian Baptism* (Philadelphia: Presbyterian and Reformed, 1970), 34.

26. Ibid., 39. Murray points out that only a true believer can honestly make such a profession. Nevertheless, even those who do not possess genuine faith may make such a profession to the satisfaction of those responsible for determining admission into the local church.

27. I am aware of one Baptist church that goes so far as to deny church membership to any preteen children who make professions of faith (and another that extends it through the teenage years), on the grounds that they might fall away from the faith when they are older and can think more independently. While this is perhaps logically consistent with the desire for a fully regenerate membership, further consistency would demand other selected proofs or tests of regeneration even for adults.

Robert Shaw, a Scottish Presbyterian minister, wrote in 1845, "But those who defer the baptism of the children of professing

Christians until they arrive at adult age, have no precedent or example for their practice; for, though the Book of Acts contains the history of the Church for upwards of thirty years, in which time the children of those who were first baptized by the apostles must have reached maturity, yet we have no record of the baptism of a single individual born of Christian parents. From this silence, we justly infer that they must have been baptized in their infancy; and we defy the advocates of adult baptism to adduce a single scriptural example of their practice" (Robert Shaw, *The Reformed Faith: An Exposition of the Westminster Confession of Faith* [Inverness: Christian Focus Publications, 1974], 290).

28. Ashbel G. Fairchild, *Scripture Baptism, Its Mode and Subjects* (Philadelphia: Presbyterian Board of Publication, 1858), 196–97.
29. Hodge, *Systematic Theology*, 3:555.

CHAPTER 6

The Covenant of Grace: Signs and Seals

THEIR COVENANT VOWS having been exchanged, Mike and Ruth neared the conclusion of their wedding ceremony. All they lacked was the exchanging of the rings and the pastor's pronouncement of "husband and wife." Pastor Williams asked the best man and the maid of honor for the rings, held them up, and addressed Mike and Ruth along with the congregation.

PASTOR WILLIAMS: These rings are a sign and seal of this marriage covenant between Mike and Ruth. They are made of gold, which represents the purity and beauty of their covenant relationship. They are made in a complete circle, representing the longevity of their covenant commitment. They are significant not only for these reasons, but also because they shall always be a sign to others that Mike and Ruth have entered into this covenant with one another. The rings are the signs and seals, the signature, the final declaration that Mike

96

and Ruth have covenantally pledged themselves, by oath, to be faithfu to one another before God as long as they both shall live. Mike, please take this ring and place it on your bride's finger and repeat after me: "With this ring I thee wed. . . ."

Mike repeated Pastor Williams's words, and Ruth did likewise. After the exchanging of the rings, Pastor Williams prayed for God's blessings on the couple and pronounced them "husband and wife."

Over the years of Mike and Ruth's marriage, their rings continually reminded them of their covenant with each other. In fact, as their relationship grew in the Lord, their rings took on even greater meaning to both of them as they realized how God had blessed them as husband and wife.

THE BANDS OF GOLD we call wedding rings do not make people married. Nevertheless, in our culture, the wedding ring has meaning attached to it. It has come to *represent the reality* of a covenant relationship between a man and a woman. It is entirely possible to be married without rings, or to wear wedding rings and not be married, or to be married, wear wedding rings, and not be faithful to the marriage vows.

Wedding rings are outward signs and seals, which, when properly used, show the inward reality of a man's and a woman's covenant commitment to one another. The person who is married and wears a wedding ring but is unfaithful to his or her spouse is a hypocrite and a covenant breaker. For those who are unfaithful, the wedding ring testifies against them. The rings are symbols of what ought to be true of those who wear them. They signify the fact that this man and this woman have been set apart for one another. Unfortunately, what ought to be true is not always so.

Circumcision and baptism are initiatory signs and seals that God chose to indicate his covenant relationship with his people. Circumcision was applied under the older covenants and baptism is applied under the new covenant. *While the form has changed,* indicating an expansion of the covenant of grace, *the meaning of the signs has remained essentially the same.* Both circumcision and baptism signify that people are born unclean and stand in need of salvation by grace. Both covenant signs set apart (i.e., make ceremonially holy) the recipient. Just as believers and their households in the Old Testament church received God's covenant sign and seal of circumcision, so too believers and their children in the new covenant church are to receive the covenant sign and seal of baptism.

Baptists generally make the dispensational assumption of a basic discontinuity between the Old and New Testaments, and divide God's people into two different groups (i.e., ethnic Israel and the spiritual church). We should not be surprised, therefore, to find them claiming that circumcision was an essentially physical or political sign and that baptism is now a spiritual sign. Some Baptists, such as David Kingdon, have conceded that such a radical dichotomy between the covenant signs cannot be maintained: "It is my considered opinion that Baptists must recognize the analogy between circumcision and baptism. It seems to me pointless to deny the existence of this analogy, yet it is often done."[1]

The dispensational system inevitably leads to denying the biblical parallel between the two signs. At best, the similarities between circumcision and baptism are thought to be coincidental and are set aside as unimportant. But we cannot untie what the Bible has so plainly tied together.

What Is a Sign and Seal?

We often make difficult what is simple. Signs and seals are no mystery—they go hand in hand. Circumcision and baptism are signs and seals in the same basic way that wedding rings are signs and seals. As signs, they signify or mean something; as seals, they confirm the binding nature of the covenant.[2]

Circumcision and baptism are signs and seals much like the signature and wax seal of the king's signet ring. The signet ring seals or confirms the genuineness of a document, much like our modern-day notary seal on a legal document. Our signature and notary seal, or the king's signature and wax seal, make an agreement or document binding and official. An unsigned or unsealed document is not valid or binding. Therefore, the words "sign" and "seal" may be used together for emphasis. Circumcision and baptism are God's *signs* in our flesh which *seal* or confirm the promise that he has made to us. Marcel elaborates on this point.

> Seals are distinct from signs in that they not only remind us of invisible things, but also authenticate these things to our religious consciousness by making them more certain and sure to us. During our daily practical life we constantly make use of seals, tokens for combating fraud, falsehood, and counterfeits. It is, in fact, necessary to distinguish the true from the false, what is authentic from what is not, the original from the counterfeit. A trade mark serves to authenticate and guarantee the source and quality of a product. Hall-marks declare the standard of alloy, the exact value, and the nationality of gold or silver articles. On weights and measures they testify to the accuracy of the inscription by reference to the scientifically determined original which they represent. Stamps, seals, and signatures guarantee the perfect authenticity of an important document—and so on. Scripture attests the usage of seals when there is a concern to prove that something is really authentic and when it is of importance to guarantee it against all falsification.[3]

The Meaning of Circumcision

The argument that circumcision had a purely natural or physical reference cannot stand the test of biblical teaching. Circumcision carried primarily a spiritual significance (i.e., justification by faith), and therefore may not be regarded as simply a physical sign of descent. It represented cleanliness (cf. Deut. 30:6; Isa. 52:1). Circumcision was an outward sign of the fact that God required a "circumcised" or cleansed heart. The Old and New Testaments are clear on this point. As Charles Hodge points out,

> That circumcision was not the sign exclusively of the national covenant with the Hebrews, is plain because it was enjoined upon Abraham and continued in practice hundreds of years before the giving of the law on Mount Sinai, when the people were inaugurated as a nation. It was instituted as the sign of the covenant . . . made with Abraham.[4]

Hodge continues, "That circumcision was not merely a civil or national institution, is further plain from its spiritual import. It signifies the cleansing from sin, just as baptism now does."[5] The Old Testament speaks of the circumcision of the heart (Deut. 10:16; Jer. 4:4; Ezek. 44:7). It tells us of uncircumcised lips that are impure lips, and of uncircumcised hearts that are unclean hearts (Ex. 6:12; Lev. 26:41; see also Acts 7:51). Paul says that the true circumcision is not that which is outward in the flesh, but that which is inward, of the heart, by the Spirit (Rom. 2:28–29). When Paul speaks of himself and other believers he says, "We are the true circumcision, who worship in the Spirit of God and glory in Christ Jesus and put no confidence in the flesh" (Phil. 3:3). Since circumcision carried such spiritual significance, its reference to the national covenant was a very subordinate matter. Its main purpose was to signify and seal the promise of deliverance from sin.[6]

Circumcision, which cut away the foreskin of the male organ of generation, constantly testified to the fact that ordinary generation was unclean and could only reproduce sinful men. Circumcision represented the removal or cutting back of that sinful nature. There was no natural hope for man's salvation.[7] Man needed to be changed and cleansed; he could not accomplish that himself. Only God could remove corruption from people's hearts, and circumcision stood as a perpetual reminder that they are dependent on the grace of God for salvation. Commenting on this fact, R. J. Rushdoony has written,

> Circumcision on the eighth day removes the power of the rite from man to God: the young child is not capable of justifying, regenerating, or sanctifying himself: he is entirely passive in the rite. The fact of divine grace is thus set forth. Just as the covenant wholly represents God's initiative and grace, so the sign of the covenant represents the same.[8]

Examining those passages which refer exclusively to circumcision, we are immediately struck with the inward and spiritual significance of the covenant sign. Leviticus 26:40–41 says,

> If they confess their iniquity and the iniquity of their forefathers, in their unfaithfulness which they committed against Me, and also in their acting with hostility against Me—I also was acting with hostility against them, to bring them into the land of their enemies—or if their uncircumcised heart becomes humbled so that they then make amends for their iniquity . . .

An uncircumcised heart is the same as one that will not confess sin and iniquity—one which refuses to repent. In other words, to have an uncircumcised heart is to be unconverted and ungodly. By implication, a regenerate and converted heart is a circumcised heart, in which there is sorrow over sin, repentance, and confession. This is the kind of heart that physical circumcision was to signify. Baptism, likewise, holds the same significance. This meaning for circumcision is seen in Deuteronomy 10:16, "Circumcise then your heart, and stiffen your neck no more," and in Deuteronomy 30:6, "Moreover the LORD your God will circumcise your heart and the heart of your descendants, to love the LORD your God with all your heart and with all your soul, in order that you may live."

Again, circumcision signified the work of God's grace in the heart, as does baptism. *The condition of the heart is at the very heart of the meaning of circumcision.* In Exodus 6:12, 30, Moses uses the term "uncircumcised" to refer to his lips being unfit to serve God before Pharaoh. In Jeremiah 4:4 and 9:25–26 we read,

> Circumcise yourselves to the LORD and remove the foreskins of your heart, men of Judah and inhabitants of Jerusalem, lest My wrath go forth like fire and burn with none to quench it, because of the evil of your deeds.

> "Behold, the days are coming," declares the LORD, "that I will punish all who are circumcised and yet uncircumcised—Egypt, and Judah, and Edom, and the sons of Ammon, and Moab, and all those inhabiting the desert who clip the hair on their temples; for all the nations are uncircumcised, and all the house of Israel are uncircumcised of heart."

God condemns those who are circumcised in the flesh, but uncircumcised of heart. These are the unrepentant men who, because of their "evil deeds," were "circumcised and yet uncircumcised." We read of the same situation in Ephesians 4:22–24, where Paul says, "Lay aside the old self, which is being corrupted in accordance with the lusts of deceit, and . . . be renewed in the spirit of your mind, and put on the new self, which in the likeness of God has been created in righteousness and holiness of the truth." Circumcision was a sign of the putting off of the old man of sin.

Romans 4:11 says, "And he [Abraham] received the sign of circumcision, a seal of the righteousness of faith which he had while uncircumcised." Circumcision was the sign that sealed the righteousness which is by faith. That is, in circumcision God signified and sealed the fact that he justifies believers by faith and considers us as righteous through faith; baptism does likewise.[9] S. H. Kellogg commented on this passage,

It is truly strange that, in the presence of these plain words of the Apostle, any should still cling to the idea that circumcision had reference only to the covenant with Israel as a nation, and not, above all, to this profound spiritual truth which is basal to salvation, whether for the Jew or for the Gentile.

And so, when the Hebrew infant was circumcised, it signified for him and for his parents these spiritual realities. It was an outward sign and seal of the covenant of God with Abraham and with his seed, to be a God to him and to his seed after him; and it signified further that this covenant of God was to be carried out and made effectual only through the putting away of the flesh, the corrupt nature with which we are born, and of all that belongs to it, in order that, thus circumcised with the circumcision of the heart, every child of Abraham might indeed be an Israelite in whom there should be no guile.[10]

From the beginning, believers and their families were the only legitimate recipients of circumcision. Circumcision without faith brought God's curse and judgment rather than his blessing. Greg Bahnsen observes,

The promises were made to Christ as *the* seed of Abraham, thus they accrue to us, Christ's brethren, as also Abraham's seed and heirs of the promise since we are Christ's (Gal. 3:29). Therefore, right from the start, the promises and their recipients did not coincide with fleshly Israel—a point which undercuts the whole outlook and circumcision requirement of the Judaizers![11]

Circumcision signified God's promise of a Redeemer, the Lamb of God, who was to come and take away the sins of his people. Circumcision was a sign and seal of God's covenant promise to believers that he was their God and that they were his people. Only in covenant faithfulness could such spiritual blessings be appropriated by the one who was circumcised. (It was still a sign and seal, even when it was not personally received by faith; covenant curses then followed). Calvin saw this when he said,

> We have, therefore, a spiritual promise given to the patriarchs in circumcision such as is given us in baptism, since it represented for them forgiveness of sins and mortification of flesh. Moreover, as we have taught that Christ is the foundation of baptism, in whom both of these reside, so it is also evident that he is the foundation of circumcision. For he is promised to Abraham, and in him the blessing of all nations [Gen. 12:2–3]. To seal this grace, the sign of circumcision is added.[12]

Undoubtedly, many Jews falsely trusted in their circumcision to grant them special favor with God, as do many today who falsely trust in their baptism. Yet, God never promised spiritual blessings to any but those who looked to him in faith.

That circumcision was primarily a religious or spiritual sign, and not one of temporal or ethnic blessing, is apparent in Scripture. Circumcision was not a requirement for participation in the national privileges of Israel. It was, however, required of those who would enter the religious aspects of the life of Israel.

In Israel, many who were uncircumcised received temporal blessings. For example, the resident alien was a foreigner who lived in the midst of Israel. He was a free man who could hire out his services (Deut. 24:14). Israelites were to show him charity and compassion (Ex. 22:21; 23:9). Aliens could glean with the rest of the poor in Israel (Lev. 19:10; 23:22), and they were under the protection of God (Deut. 10:18). Israelites were to love aliens as they loved themselves (Lev. 19:34). The alien could share in the poor tithe (Deut. 14:29) and in the Sabbatical year (Lev. 25:6). He was entitled to the protection of the cities of refuge (Num. 35:15) and to the same legal rights as Israelites (Deut. 1:16). However, aliens were not to partake of the Passover unless they had been circumcised (Ex. 12:48–49). This emphasizes the religious and spiritual significance of circumcision. Richard P. Flinn comments,

> But if all these advantages were enjoyed by the uncircumcised as well as the circumcised, except for the passover, we are justified in concluding that these external, temporal blessings and privileges were not the heart of the Old Covenant. The essence of the Covenant remains ethical and religious.[13]

Circumcision, far from being a sign of ethnicity, was essentially a spiritual sign and seal that set God's people apart. It focused on the need for repentance and a believing, cleansed heart. It pointed to the necessity of spiritual regeneration—natural generation could produce nothing but corruption. Circumcision united God's people to his promised Redeemer, Jesus Christ, and secured their position as his people forever. Yet, without covenant faithfulness, the outward sign of circumcision brought no blessing and led only to curses on the covenant breaker. As a sinner, Abraham was saved by grace. And God called for him to receive the sign and seal of this salvation—circumcision. As a believer, Abraham was then to apply this sign and seal of salvation to his household, including his infant children.

The Meaning of Baptism

We have seen the spiritual significance of the covenant sign and seal of circumcision. We now turn to examine the biblical evidence for the significance and meaning of baptism.[14]

In the book of Acts we read, "And Peter said to them, 'Repent, and let each of you be baptized in the name of Jesus Christ for the forgiveness of your sins; and you shall receive the gift of the Holy Spirit'" (2:38). And Paul is quoted as saying, "And now why do you delay? Arise, and be baptized, and wash away your sins, calling on His name" (22:16).

In these passages we see that baptism signifies or represents repentance and the remission of sins. Baptism itself washes away no sins. It does, however, represent the washing away of sins. This general declaration of redemptive truth is not a specific testimony about the one who is baptized. As in the Old Testament, a clean heart is required for God's people in the new covenant.

Another facet of baptism is seen in Romans 6:4: "Therefore we have been buried with Him through baptism into death, in order that as Christ was raised from the dead through the glory of the Father, so we too might walk in newness of life." Like circumcision, baptism is the sign of spiritual renewal in Christ; both point to regeneration. Baptism offers nothing new at this point. *Circumcision looked forward to the saving work of the Redeemer; baptism looks back on his completed work on the cross.* The Old Testament believer was taught about the need for, and the gracious provision of, renewal in circumcision as he expected the fulfillment of God's promises. The new covenant believer finds renewal in baptism as he considers that God has fulfilled the promise that he made to Abraham (Gal. 3:14). This is expressed again in Galatians 3:27–29, where we see that baptism places one in the Abrahamic covenant.

> For all of you who were baptized into Christ have clothed yourselves with Christ. There is neither Jew nor Greek, there is neither slave nor free man, there is neither male nor female; for you are all one in Christ Jesus. And if you belong to Christ, then you are Abraham's offspring, heirs according to promise.

The circumcision and baptism of believers and their children demonstrate that salvation is from the hand of God alone and that all men are helpless to save themselves. All men stand in need of regeneration and purification, and the covenant signs and seals clearly show this need. B. B. Warfield emphasizes that baptism is a picture of grace: "Every time we baptize an infant we bear witness that salvation is from God, that we cannot do any good thing to secure it, that we receive it from his hands as a sheer gift of his grace, and that we all enter the Kingdom of heaven therefore as little children, who do not do, but are done for."[15]

Baptism, like circumcision, is essentially a spiritual sign and seal that sets us apart as God's people. It too signifies the need for, and God's gracious provision of, a renewed and cleansed heart. It points to the necessity of spiritual regeneration. Baptism unites believers and their children with God's promised Redeemer, Jesus Christ, and secures their position as his people. Baptism must also be responded to by faith before covenant blessings may be appropriated. Failure to faithfully respond to one's baptism brings covenant curses rather than blessings.[16]

Circumcision and Baptism Are Alike

To further demonstrate that circumcision and baptism carry essentially the same meaning, we turn to those passages of Scripture which equate the two. Colossians 2:11–12 says,

> And in Him you were also circumcised with a circumcision made without hands, in the removal of the body of the flesh by the circumcision of Christ; having been buried with Him in baptism, in which you were also raised up with Him through faith in the working of God, who raised Him from the dead.

In this passage, Paul clearly identifies the signs of circumcision and baptism with each other. As he writes to the church of the new covenant, he explains that believers are circumcised in the spiritual sense of that word, and that this spiritual circumcision takes place as they are buried with Christ in baptism. This equating of the essential meaning of circumcision and baptism could not be any clearer. *Just as physical circumcision indicated a circumcision of the heart, so now physical baptism indicates a circumcision of the heart.*

We similarly read in Philippians 3:3, "For we are the true circumcision, who worship in the Spirit of God and glory in Christ Jesus and put no confidence in the flesh." Here the apostle does not mention baptism or even allude to it. Yet, he maintains that Christians, who have been baptized, rather than unbelieving Jews, are those who have been truly circumcised. The meaning of circumcision has not been discarded but continues in the church of the new covenant and is signified by baptism.[17]

When baptism was implemented, circumcision was no longer necessary as a sign. The apostles did permit Jewish Christian infants to be circumcised under the new covenant, but they decided that it would be inappropriate for the Gentiles (cf. Acts 21:18–25).[18] If the infants of Jewish Christians were permitted to receive the covenant sign of circumcision, and thereby enter the covenant, so too would the infants of Gentile believers be eligible to receive the covenant sign of baptism and thereby enter the covenant.

Professor John Murray lays out the three primary ideas that are central to both circumcision and baptism: First, they signify union and communion with God; at the very heart of each covenant administration is the simple declaration, "I shall be their God, and they shall be my people."[19] Second, they signify the removal of defilement; before there can be union and communion with God, man must be cleansed from defilement. Both circumcision and baptism outwardly signify the necessary inward cleansing.[20] Third, they signify the righteousness of faith. Paul says that circumcision was administered to Abraham as a seal of the righteousness received by him through faith.[21] Likewise, baptism signifies the righteousness of faith, that is, justification by faith.[22]

Calvin drew this conclusion:

Now we can see without difficulty the similarity and difference of these two signs. The promise (in which we have shown the power of the signs to consist) is the same in both, namely, that of God's fatherly favor, of forgiveness of sins, and of eternal life. Then the thing represented is the same, namely, regeneration. In both there is one foundation upon which the fulfillment of these things rests. . . . What dissimilarity remains lies in the outward ceremony, which is a very slight factor, since the most weighty part depends upon the promise and the thing signified. We therefore conclude that, apart from the difference in the visible ceremony, whatever belongs to circumcision pertains likewise to baptism. . . . And the thing is so true we can almost touch it. For circumcision was for the Jews their first entry into the church, because it was a token to them by which they were assured of adoption as the people and household of God, and they in turn professed to enlist in God's service. In like manner, we also are consecrated to God through baptism, to be reckoned as his people, and in turn we swear fealty to him. By this it appears incontrovertible that baptism has taken the place of circumcision to fulfill the same office among us.[23]

John Flavel also noted this parallel between the infants of Old and New Testament believers when he said,

Nor can the subtlest enemy to infant baptism give us a convincing reason why the infants of Gentile believers are not equally capable of the same benefits that the infants of Jewish believers were, if they still stand under the same covenant that the former stood under; and God hath no where repealed the gracious grant formerly made to the infant-seed of his covenant-people.[24]

This clear connection between the two covenant signs of circumcision and baptism creates a difficult problem for the opponents of infant baptism, for *any argument against infant baptism is necessarily an argument against infant circumcision.* Any objection raised against the inclusion of the infants of believers in the covenant can be answered with, "Because it pleased the

Lord to do so." Calvin commented on the command of God to include the infants of believers among his covenant people:

> For it is very clear from many testimonies of Scripture that circumcision was also a sign of repentance [Jer. 4:4; 9:25; cf. Deut. 10:16; 30:6]. Then Paul calls it the seal of the righteousness of faith [Rom. 4:11]. Therefore, let a reason be required of God himself why he commanded it to be impressed on the bodies of infants. For since baptism and circumcision are in the same case, our opponents cannot give anything to one without conceding it to the other. . . . [S]ince God communicated circumcision to infants as a sacrament of repentance and of faith, it does not seem absurd if they are now made participants in baptism. . . .
>
> . . . God's command concerning circumcision of infants was either lawful and not to be trifled with, or it was deserving of censure. If there was in it nothing incongruous or absurd, neither can anything absurd be found in the observance of infant baptism.[25]

To further demonstrate that baptism replaced circumcision as the covenant sign of redemption, John P. Sartelle proposes that we answer these three questions:

1. When a person believed in the God of Abraham and trusted in Him in the Old Testament, what happened?

   He was circumcised.

2. What was the outward event that represented the clean heart in the Old Testament?

   Circumcision.

3. What was the outward sign that marked a person's entrance into the community of believers in the Old Testament?

   Circumcision.

Sartelle then suggests that we ask these same questions, replacing the words "Old Testament" with "New Testament":

1. When a person believed in the God of Abraham and trusted in Him in the New Testament, what happened?

   He was baptized.

2. What was the external event that represented the clean heart in the New Testament?

   Baptism.

3. What was the outward sign that marked a person's entrance into the community of believers in the New Testament?

   Baptism.[26]

Why Change Circumcision to Baptism?

Reformed paedobaptists agree that the new covenant brought significant changes to the history of redemption. However, these changes were not so significant as to invalidate the principles of the older covenants. Yet, the new covenant did expand upon the previous covenant administrations and usher in a greater degree of blessing, thus extending the application of these blessings to more people than before. There was a greater outpouring of the Holy Spirit (Acts 2:17). Gentiles were now included on a par with Jews (Gal. 3:14), and women now received equal covenant privilege (Gal. 3:28). These and other blessings were not minor changes; they called for fresh signs that would draw attention to the new circumstances.

Many of the burdensome rites of the Old Testament were changed under the new covenant to reflect the completed work of Christ (e.g., no more animal sacrifices). Thanks to the work of Christ, a few simple ordinances were put in their place.[27] Water baptism replaced the bloody rite of circumcision, just as the bread and wine replaced the bloody Passover lamb.[28] The shed blood of Christ meant that there was no longer any need for blood to be shed in order for his people to be cleansed and made pure. Under the new covenant, God's people had greater revelation and understanding of his redemptive work. It pleased God for the water of baptism, and the bread and wine of the Lord's Supper, to mark the fact that his redemptive work was now completed and that there was no longer any need for blood to be shed.

Misunderstanding of Baptism

One difference between Baptists and Reformed paedobaptists has been the baptistic notion that baptism is the subjective testimony of the individual believer—his profession of faith—"the Christian man's badge of profession." The Scriptures indicate that the covenant is sovereignly initiated by God, not by man, and therefore that the covenant sign and seal is God's, not the believer's. It is God's message (sign), not man's. It is applied to the believer and his household by God to signify his claims on the person or household as set apart unto him. They are marked out as a people for God's own possession. B. B. Warfield explained,

> Baptism, as circumcision, is a gift of God to his people, not of his people to God. Abraham did not bring circumcision to God; he "received" it from God. God gave it to him as a "sign" and a "seal," not to others but to himself. It is inadequate, therefore, to speak of baptism as "the badge of a Christian man's profession." . . . The witness of baptism is not to others but to ourselves; and it is not by us but by God that the witness is borne.[29]

Baptists have argued that baptism is a sign and seal of faith, regeneration, and the forgiveness of sin, and therefore may only be administered to those whom we know to be believers—only those who profess genuine faith. They go on to argue that since many infants who are baptized do not profess genuine faith later in life—and, in fact, demonstrate via ungodly lives that they are indeed not the children of God—clearly the sign of baptism should not be administered to the children of believers before they come to an age of understanding.[30] With this argument Baptists unwittingly argue against infant circumcision, which the Lord clearly required to be administered to Abraham's children.

Like baptism, circumcision was a sign of the righteousness that is by faith, a picture of spiritual circumcision, or circumcision of the heart. Circumcision was a sign of regeneration and sanctification, the cutting away of the old man of sin, and of a new heart that loves God. In all these ways, the significance of the old covenant sign of circumcision was the same as the new covenant sign of baptism.[31]

The fact that someone belonged to God was evidenced by the mark of circumcision. It was the sign that separated God's people from the Gentile world. We are told in Exodus 12:48, "If a stranger sojourns with you, and celebrates the Passover to the LORD, let all his males be circumcised, and then let him come near to celebrate it; and he shall be like a native of the land. But no uncircumcised person may eat of it."

Likewise, baptism is now the sign that separates God's people from the world. Former Baptist turned Presbyterian theologian James Henley Thornwell points out the advantages that circumcised or baptized persons have over the rest of the world.

> Their baptism has brought them, as contradistinguished from others, into the same relation to the promises of the covenant into which circumcision brought the Jew as contradistinguished from the Gentile. To them belong in a special sense, the Oracles of God, and "to them pertain the adoption, and the glory, and the covenants, and the giving of the law, and the service of God, and the promises." They can plead the promises as an unbaptized sinner cannot plead them. God is nigh to them

for all that they call upon him for. The Scriptures evidently distinguish unbelievers into two great classes—those who are *nigh*, and those who are *afar off*. These terms do not express, so much, differences of moral character as different relations to the covenant.[32]

It cannot be overstated that baptism is not man's testimony, but God's testimony. Baptism is not intended as the testimony of the one being baptized that he has personally repented and believed. In fact, baptism is not a sign of anything we do. It is a sign of God's work on our behalf, by means of his gracious covenant, to save his elect people. It is a sign of God's calling. Repentance and faith are responses to this initiating call of God. Greg Bahnsen comments,

> Abraham's circumcision was God's testimony in Abraham's flesh that righteousness cannot be merited by man's natural efforts—that it must be graciously imputed to the helpless sinner. Abraham was reckoned righteous, therefore, only by trusting in God's promise and provision—faith. . . . We must note well that the signs of the covenant, whether circumcision or baptism,—being God's signs and ordained by Him—are God's testimony to God's gracious work of salvation. They declare the objective truth that justification comes only by faith in God's promise. Circumcision and baptism are not an individual's personal, subjective testimony to having saving faith for himself. God Himself commanded that circumcision be applied to those whom He perfectly well knew would not have saving faith in Him (e.g., Ishmael in Gen. 17:18–27).[33]

What Does This Have to Do with Infant Baptism?

The parallels between circumcision and baptism are undeniable. If the meaning of both signs is essentially the same, and God commanded infants to be circumcised under the old covenant, then it follows that, unless God expressly forbids infant inclusion in the new covenant, infants should also be baptized. This becomes even more evident when we consider that the new covenant administration is an extension of the Abrahamic covenant and the fulfillment of its promise.

The old covenant administrations are but the bud, and the new covenant administration is the full flowering of God's promise. If infants were included when the promise was first made to Abraham, how can we believe, without an express command, that they are to be excluded when the promise has come to full fruition?[34]

May we justly conclude that the new covenant is less inclusive and less generous than the old, especially when we consider that baptism signifies the same covenant blessings as circumcision? While the New Testament provides a greater revelation and a sharper definition of just what those blessings are and exactly how we attain them, these are not different kinds of blessings in themselves. For such a radical change in the administration of the covenant of grace to have occurred, there must be a clear revocation of the practice commanded by the Word of God. That is especially required since the new covenant is built upon, and finds its meaning in, the fulfillment of the Abrahamic covenant and promise.[35] But there is no evidence of such a revocation in the pages of Scripture. As Robert L. Dabney said, "The change of dispensation is the change of outward form, not of its substance or nature." Nowhere do we see a repeal of God's everlasting covenant with Abraham.[36]

We must appreciate that circumcision required understanding by its recipient if it was to be a blessing to him, and yet God commanded it to be administered to infants. The same situation applies to Christian baptism. Infants are still included in the covenant, but the outward form of the covenant sign and seal has been changed to water baptism. As R. C. Sproul has observed, "The crucial point is that in the Old Testament, God ordered that a sign of faith be given *before* faith was present. Since that was clearly the case, it is erroneous to argue *in principle* that it is wrong to administer a sign of faith before faith is present."[37]

Because they are the initiatory signs and seals of the covenant of grace, circumcision and baptism carry essentially the same meaning in Scripture. They are both outward signs of the inward, spiritual need for the grace of God in the heart of the covenant member. Both signs unite the recipient with God's promised Redeemer, Jesus Christ. Like circumcision in the Old Testament, baptism in the New Testament is to be administered to believers and their children to mark them out and set them apart as the people of God. To oppose infant baptism now is to oppose infant circumcision in the Old Testament. Calvin warned, "If it enters anyone's mind to jest at infant baptism on this pretext, he is mocking the command of circumcision given by the Lord. For what will they bring forward to impugn infant baptism that may not be turned back against circumcision?"[38]

God delights believers and blesses them by blessing those closest to them—their households, their children. Circumcision and baptism bring comfort and delight to believers' hearts as they consider their covenant-keeping God. These signs seal God's promises to the hearts of believers and their children. Calvin summarized this blessing to God's people:

> For this holy institution of his, by which we feel our faith singularly comforted, does not deserve to be called superfluous. For God's sign, communicated to a child as by an impressed seal, confirms the promise given to the pious parent, and declares it to be ratified that the Lord will be God not only to him but to his seed; and that he wills to manifest his goodness and grace not only to him but to his descendants even to the thousandth generation [Ex. 20:6]. God's boundless generosity, in showing itself there, first gives men ample occasion to proclaim his glory, then floods godly hearts with uncommon happiness, which quickens men to a deeper love of their kind Father, as they see his concern on their behalf for their posterity.[39]

NOTES

1. David Kingdon, *Children of Abraham* (London: Carey Publications, 1975), 28.
2. The Greek word for "sign" (*semeion*) means "a mark or token by which anything is known or distinguished; a pledge, assurance, proof, or evidence." The Greek word for "seal" (*sphragis*) means "a signet ring; a token or a guarantee; that which confirms, attests, authenticates, or places beyond doubt."
3. Pierre Ch. Marcel, *The Biblical Doctrine of Infant Baptism* (Cambridge: James Clarke, 1981), 30. Marcel notes, "Scripture informs us that seals were placed on the letters of princes (1 Kings 21:8; Neh. 9:38; Esth. 3:12) or of other persons (Jer. 32:10), on laws which had been promulgated (Isa. 8:16), or on important books (Dan. 12:4; Rev. 22:10). In order to safeguard them from all interference the den of lions of Daniel (Dan. 6:18) and Christ's tomb (Matt. 27:66ff.) were sealed."
4. Charles Hodge, *Systematic Theology* (Grand Rapids: Eerdmans, 1991), 3:553–54.
5. Ibid., 554–55.
6. Ibid., 555.
7. Greg L. Bahnsen, "Baptism: Its Meaning and Purpose" (Auburn, Calif.: Covenant Tape Ministry, 1987), 3.
8. R. J. Rushdoony, *The Institutes of Biblical Law* (Nutley, N.J.: Craig Press, 1973), 1:42.
9. Herman Hoeksema, *Triple Knowledge: An Exposition of the Heidelberg Catechism* (Grand Rapids: Reformed Free Publishing, 1971), 540–41.
10. S. H. Kellogg, *Studies in Leviticus* (1891; reprint, Grand Rapids: Kregel, 1988), 327.
11. Greg L. Bahnsen, *Theonomy in Christian Ethics*, 2d ed. (Phillipsburg, N.J.: Presbyterian and Reformed, 1984), 507.
12. John Calvin, *Institutes of the Christian Religion*, ed. John T. McNeill (Philadelphia: Westminster Press, 1960), 2:1327.
13. Richard P. Flinn, "Baptism, Redemptive History, and Eschatology: The Parameters of Debate," in *The Failure of the American Baptist Culture*, ed. James B. Jordan, Christianity and Civilization, no. 1 (Tyler, Tex.: Geneva Divinity School, 1982), 141–42. Who are the children of believers in the new covenant more like: the aliens in Israel or the children of old covenant believers?

14. Remember, the foundation for every teaching in the New Testament is found in the Old Testament—e.g., the sacrifice of Christ and animal sacrifice, the Lord's Supper and the Passover meal, and now baptism and circumcision.

15. Benjamin B. Warfield, *Selected Shorter Writings* (Nutley, N.J.: Presbyterian and Reformed, 1970), 1:329.

16. Bahnsen ("Baptism: Its Meaning and Purpose," 4) has pointed out, "God Himself commanded that circumcision be applied to those whom He perfectly well knew would not have saving faith in Him (e.g., Ishmael in Gen. 17:18–27). Likewise, in plenty of instances hypocrites who are not true believers have been baptized (cf. Heb. 6:2–6; e.g., Simon Magus in Acts 8:13, 20–23). Some might object that, while God knowingly applied a sign of the Old Covenant to unbelievers (like Ishmael or Esau), this would be inappropriate in the New Covenant. They say New Covenant signs are only for those we have reason to think are believers (by their profession of faith). Such reasoning is well meaning, but nonetheless unbiblical. God the Son knowingly applied the sign of even the New Covenant to the unbelieving 'son of perdition,' Judas Iscariot (Luke 22:20–21; Matt. 26:23–29)."

17. Hoeksema, *Triple Knowledge*, 542.

18. In Acts 21:18–25, Paul is slandered by the Jews for allegedly teaching that they were "not to circumcise their children." This certainly would have been an appropriate time for the apostles to point out that children were no longer to be included in the covenant, if that were so. Rather than disapproving of infant inclusion in the covenant, the apostles confirmed their approval of the practice. Gentile believers, being on equal footing with Jewish believers, would have their children received into the covenant by way of baptism. See Douglas Wilson, *To a Thousand Generations: Covenant Mercy, Infant Baptism, and the People of God*, 19–28 (forthcoming from Canon Press, P.O. Box 8741, Moscow, ID 83843, 800-488-2034).

19. Cf. Gen. 17:7; Ex. 19:5–6; Deut. 7:6; Jer. 31:33; Heb. 8:10.

20. Cf. Ex. 6:12, 30; Lev. 19:23; 26:41; Deut. 10:16; 30:6; Jer. 4:4; 6:10; 9:25; Acts 2:38; 22:16; Col. 2:13.

21. Cf. Rom. 4:11; also Rom. 2:25–29; Col. 2:11–14; Phil. 3:2–3.

22. John Murray, *Christian Baptism* (Philadelphia: Presbyterian and Reformed, 1970), 50–51.

23. Calvin, *Institutes*, 2:1327.

24. John Flavel, *The Works of John Flavel* (reprint, London: Banner of Truth, 1968), 3:544–45.
25. Calvin, *Institutes*, 2:1342–44.
26. John P. Sartelle, *Infant Baptism: What Christian Parents Should Know* (Phillipsburg, N.J.: Presbyterian and Reformed, 1985), 10–11.
27. The Westminster Confession of Faith, chap. 7, sec. 6, says, "Under the gospel, when Christ, the substance, was exhibited, the ordinances in which this covenant is dispensed are the preaching of the Word, and the administration of the sacraments of Baptism and the Lord's Supper: which, though fewer in number, and administered with more simplicity, and less outward glory, yet, in them, it is held forth in more fullness, evidence, and spiritual efficacy, to all nations, both Jews and Gentiles; and is called the new testament. There are not therefore two covenants of grace, differing in substance, but one and the same, under various dispensations."
28. Since water is the universal cleaning agent, we can see why God chose it to be the sign of inward cleansing.
29. Warfield, *Selected Shorter Writings*, 1:327.
30. Hoeksema, *Triple Knowledge*, 539.
31. Ibid., 540.
32. James Henley Thornwell, *The Collected Writings of James Henley Thornwell*, ed. B. M. Palmer (Carlisle, Pa.: Banner of Truth, 1986), 4:330.
33. Bahnsen, "Baptism: Its Meaning and Purpose," 3–4.
34. Murray, *Christian Baptism*, 52–53.
35. Ibid.
36. Robert L. Dabney, *Lectures in Systematic Theology* (1878; reprint, Grand Rapids: Zondervan, 1972), 781.
37. R. C. Sproul, *Essential Truths of the Christian Faith* (Wheaton, Ill.: Tyndale House, 1992), 228.
38. Calvin, *Institutes*, 2:1331–32.
39. Ibid., 1332.

CHAPTER 7

Households and Redemption: To Your Children and Your Children's Children

RICK TAUGHT HIGH SCHOOL HISTORY, and so he often talked about history with his six-year-old son Keith as he drove him to school in the morning. One morning Rick was describing to Keith what it was like when the American pioneers were moving westward toward the frontier. Rick thought he would quiz Keith to see how much he understood.

> RICK: Hey, buddy, can you tell me when the pioneers lived?
> KEITH: A long, long time ago.
> RICK: Why were they going west?
> KEITH: Because they wanted their own land.
> RICK: That's right. What kind of cars did they drive?
> KEITH: They had real big cars so they could take all the stuff they needed.

RICK: I asked you a trick question. The pioneers didn't have cars. Cars had not even been invented yet. The pioneers used horses and oxen to pull wagons.

KEITH: Oh, yeah. I forgot about that.

Rick and Keith had a good laugh about "pioneer station wagons" as Rick dropped Keith off at school.

CHILDREN ARE NOT the only ones prone to make the mistake Keith made. It is easy for any of us to assume that other peoples and cultures have understood life the same way we do now. It is important for us to consider how people thought in the first-century Mediterranean world. Did people then see the world primarily as individuals, or did they view their world in terms of entire households and covenantal units? We need to understand the historical context of God's revelation if we are to grasp the doctrines of Scripture, including the doctrine of baptism.

I have shown the continuity of the covenant of grace, the continuity of the church, and the continuity between circumcision and baptism—these are the foundational arguments. We come now to consider some supporting evidence for infant baptism. While this evidence does not, by itself, deductively prove the truth of infant baptism (which has already been demonstrated), it does lend strong inductive support to the doctrine. It is supporting evidence that should not be surprising to find in Scripture, considering the full testimony of God's covenantal Word. I am referring to the covenant household, which demonstrates the beauty of including infants in the covenant of grace.

An appreciation of the household unit and of the corporate reality of the family is vital to a biblical understanding of redemption. Baptists have emphasized the importance of the individual believer to the point where all other redemptive concerns have faded in significance. It is difficult for someone in an individualistic culture, such as our own, to comprehend the importance of corporate and familial structures. "After all," it is argued, "in the end, the only thing that matters is individual and personal salvation." But the Bible's view of redemption is not that narrow.

God's redemptive purposes are much broader than the individual—they include every area of life. Further, it is not necessary that the individual always appreciate why something is important. If God says it is important, then that is sufficient reason for the believer to practice it. As we mature in knowledge and grace, we may come to appreciate the reasons behind God's redemptive plans.

The Old Testament Concept of the Household

To understand the New Testament passages that refer to "households," we must examine the Old Testament concept of the household. Some writers, such as the Baptist Alexander Carson, have argued that we have no real scriptural precedent for the idea of a household and are therefore free to define it however we wish.[1] While it is understandable that he wishes to have such liberty, we cannot go along with him. The Bible must be studied for the proper understanding of its crucial concepts.

Scripture is full of definitive examples in which households are understood as including all those who are under the authority of the head of a covenantal family unit. A household could include not only a husband, his wife, and their children, but also any slaves.[2] As the head of the household went, so went the family, every member being affected. We cannot agree with the Baptist theologian A. H. Strong that "the notion that the family is the unit of society is a relic of barbarism."[3] The biblical emphasis on the family unit is anything but barbaric.

Old Testament society was ordered by God and was dominated by a family and tribal structure. It was a patriarchal society that depended on the head of the household for everything. Adam represented not only himself, but also his posterity. Noah went into the ark with "all his house" (Gen. 7:1). The Lord "plagued Pharaoh and his house" (Gen. 12:17). "All" who were "born in Abraham's house" or who were "bought with his money" were to be circumcised (Gen. 17:12–13, 23, 27). God spared Lot and his household from the destruction of Sodom (Gen. 19:16). The Lord "closed fast all the wombs of the household of Abimelech" because of Abimelech's sin (Gen. 20:17–18). As a result of the sin of Simeon and Levi, Jacob said, "I shall be destroyed, I and my household" (Gen. 34:30). Households were spared death where the blood of the Passover lamb was applied to their doorposts (Ex. 12:27). The Levites were numbered according to their household membership (Num. 3:15). Joshua spoke for his entire household when he declared, "As for me and my house, we will serve the LORD" (Josh. 24:15). God judged the house of Eli because of the sins of his sons (1 Sam. 3:12–14). David brought God's judgment upon his whole house because of his sinful conduct with Bathsheba (2 Sam. 12:10). There are hundreds of references in the Old Testament to "houses" or "households" that clearly include all members born in those families and all who were adopted or who were owned by those families as slaves.

In the Old Testament (and in the New), the parent-child relationship is organic; that is, God views parents and children not simply as individuals that happen to be related but as a divinely created unit or organism. This organism extends through the generations. We find the principle of the organic unity of the family illustrated in the pages of Scripture, both negatively and positively. In Joshua 7:15, 24–25, we see a negative example, in that not only Achan but also his entire family with him were stoned for his theft of silver and gold. God promised to punish the wicked, "visiting the iniquity of fathers on the children and on the grandchildren to the third and fourth generations" (Ex. 34:7).[4]

The New Testament Concept of the Household

The Old Testament concept of the household continues in the New Testament, which has many references to households. For example, an elder "must be one who manages his own household well, keeping his children under control with all dignity" (1 Tim. 3:4). Likewise, deacons must be "good managers of their children and their own households" (1 Tim. 3:12). Elders must have "children who believe" (Titus 1:6). Surely we are not to suppose that this requirement for church officers excludes those who have small children and only embraces those whose children are old enough to be counted as adults.

In Philippians 4:22 we are told of the saints who were "of Caesar's household." These saints were probably Caesar's slaves, yet they were considered to be a part of his household. Biblical usage determines the meaning of biblical terms. We may not arbitrarily redefine a term simply because it creates theological problems for our preconceived notions. Those who would exclude children and slaves from the term "household" must go against the overwhelming testimony of Scripture.

A centurion once came to Jesus on behalf of his servant who was paralyzed and suffering (Matt. 8:5–13). The Lord commended the centurion for his faith, and as a result he healed the servant. There is no indication that the servant had anything to do with this. However, since the servant was a member of the centurion's household, he benefited from the centurion's faith.[5]

As a child, whenever I heard the story of Jesus feeding the four thousand, the Sunday school teacher was quick to point out that in the days of Jesus only the heads of households were counted. Therefore, there were really many more than 4,000 people fed by Jesus: "And those who ate were four thousand men, besides women and children" (Matt. 15:38).

This makes sense in a household-oriented society. We see this again in Peter's sermon on the day of Pentecost, when he addressed the "men of Judea" (Acts 2:14) and the "men of Israel" (v. 22) as his "brethren" (v. 29). These men asked Peter and the apostles, "What shall we do?" (v. 37). Peter's reply to these heads of households was, "Repent, and let each of you be baptized in the name of Jesus Christ for the forgiveness of your sins; and you shall receive the gift of the Holy Spirit. For the promise is for you and your children, and for all who are far off, as many as the Lord our God shall call to Himself" (vv. 38–

39). The fact that Peter addressed heads of households in this sermon at the inauguration of the new covenant demonstrates that first-century Jews, like their Old Testament predecessors, thought and functioned in terms of households. Individualism would have to wait until the time of the Renaissance.[6]

Parents Represent Their Children

The infants of believers do not make a conscious choice when they are baptized into the covenant of grace. Nor are they expected to do so. The head of the household obligates them to carry out the terms of the covenant. He is in fact authorized and required to do so as the organic head of the family. Genesis 17:14 says, "But an uncircumcised male who is not circumcised in the flesh of his foreskin, that person shall be cut off from his people; he has broken my covenant."

The adult or child who is uncircumcised is a covenant breaker. But how could God blame a child, who is not yet aware of his actions, for the failure of his parents to secure the covenant sign? God does so because he views the family as an organic unit, in which, if the head sins, all the parts of the organism are held to be sinful with it.[7]

The family or household, as a social unit, looms large on the pages of Scripture. God's covenantal dealings are always manifest in terms of their effects upon the family, both negatively and positively. A. A. Hodge observes, "The Church had its beginnings in the family. The plan of redemption assumes and presumes the original state of human beings as in the family."[8]

Since children were members of the Abrahamic covenant, we must assume that they continue to be members of the new covenant (there being no command in the New Testament to exclude them). God has consistently dealt with households in every age and has embraced children along with their parents. We see this in the covenant made with Adam (and in the curse that followed because of its violation), in the covenant with Noah, in the judgment upon Sodom, in the destruction

of the Canaanites and Amalekites, in the whole structure of
society, and in the governments ordained by God. In all these,
the infant children go where the parents go. If the church were
different in this respect, it would certainly be an oddity.[9]

This point is confirmed by the fact that within the New
Testament letters written to the church, portions are addressed
to the constituent members of the traditional household—husbands, wives, parents, children, and slaves. For example, we
read in Colossians 3:18–22,

> *Wives*, be subject to your husbands, as is fitting in the
> Lord. *Husbands*, love your wives, and do not be embit-
> tered against them. *Children*, be obedient to your par-
> ents in all things, for this is well-pleasing to the Lord.
> *Fathers*, do not exasperate your children, that they may
> not lose heart. *Slaves*, in all things obey those who are
> your masters on earth, not with external service, as those
> who merely please men, but with sincerity of heart, fear-
> ing the Lord.

When the Bible speaks of a household, it includes every
member of the family—husband, wife, children (including infants), and slaves. Kenneth Gentry expresses the biblical principle of family solidarity in God's covenantal dealings when he
observes, "There is *nothing* in the New Testament that under-
mines and invalidates the Old Testament covenantal principle
of family solidarity. In fact, everything confirms its continuing
validity. Thus, a covenantal understanding of baptism leads
inexorably to infant baptism."[10]

The Redemptive Purpose of the Family

The corporate redemptive concerns of God have always embraced the families of God's people, as well as the other areas
of their lives. But it is especially evident in Scripture that God
has a special place for the children of his people. He loves
believers, and he loves the children of believers. As a result,

the Lord pours out many blessings upon believing households, as seen in both the old and new covenants.

The Bible calls for a broad understanding of God's redemptive purposes. The new covenant embraces the entire human society. Many instructions govern and redeem our relationships in the church. Even relationships with those outside the church fall under these redemptive regulations (Rom. 12:19–21). The new covenant redeems and reconstructs the family and gives many material blessings (Mark 10:29–30). Fathers, mothers, husbands, wives, and children are all instructed by the new covenant Scriptures (Eph. 5:22–6:4; Col. 3:18–21). The God-ordained institutions of marriage and parenthood are to be reformed and reconstructed continually until they reach Christian maturity.[11]

We are told in Malachi 2:15 that one purpose for the institution of the marriage covenant and the family was "to seek a godly seed," that is, to provide for the raising of godly children. Robert L. Dabney noted that it would be strange for the church not to completely embrace the family as a subdivision of itself. In view of the influences of the parents, their affection and authority, it would seem incredible that God would omit them as instruments of his grace to their children. Parental love is the strongest of instincts, reflecting God's own love and patience. There is no authority delegated to man that is any stronger than parental authority. Parents have influence over their children's intelligence, culture, and religious beliefs. In fact, a child's disposition toward God is influenced by his parents more than by anyone else. Has God omitted this instrument in constituting his church?[12]

The households of believers have played a prominent role in redemptive history. On what grounds would we expect that God no longer sees believers' households redemptively? At what point did God shift his love and concern away from our children? Church historian William Cunningham noted,

> In the whole history of our race, God's covenanted dealings with His people, with respect to spiritual blessings,

have had regard to their children as well as to themselves; so that the children as well as the parents have been admitted to the spiritual blessings of God's covenants, and to the outward signs and seals of these covenants; . . . there is no evidence that this general principle, so full of mercy and grace, and so well fitted to nourish faith and hope, was to be departed from, or laid aside, under the Christian dispensation; but, on the contrary, a great deal to confirm the conviction that it was to continue to be acted on.[13]

We must not forget that once God has spoken concerning any matter, including spiritual privileges, his word cannot be altered, revoked, or annulled without the further revelation of God himself. God has, throughout redemptive history, expanded the scope of his privileges and blessings. He granted the spiritual privilege of participating in the covenant and of receiving the initial covenant sign to the entire household of Abraham (including his infant children, Gen. 17:10–12). This privilege must stand forever, unless God expressly revokes it or replaces it with a greater privilege. But rather than including the children of believers in God's visible covenant community, Baptists place their children in the pagan community.[14] In the words of Puritan theologian John Owen,

> All this contest, therefore, is to deprive the children of believers of a privilege once granted them by God, never revoked, as to the substance of it, assigning nothing in its room; which is contrary to the goodness, love, and covenant of God, especially derogatory to the honour of Jesus Christ and the gospel.[15]

Believers and Their Households

It was believers, along with their households, who were to receive the covenant sign of circumcision in the Old Testament. These believers, who possessed the same faith as Abraham, were the true seed of Abraham. The apostle Paul declares, "They are not all Israel who are descended from Israel" (Rom. 9:6). Likewise, in the New Testament, it is those who trust in the promise God made to Abraham who are considered his true seed. "That is, it is not the children of the flesh who are children of God, but the children of the promise are regarded as descendants" (Rom. 9:8; cf. Gal. 3:7–9). So also, the new covenant believer, being the true seed of Abraham, brings his entire household into covenant with God, and his household receives the covenant sign.[16]

It is not true that only the physical descendants of Abraham were circumcised. When a Gentile adopted the Jewish faith, he received the covenant sign and seal in his flesh, thus becoming the seed of Abraham. Moreover, all the male members of his household were also circumcised, even if they had not personally believed (Ex. 12:48–49; cf. Gal. 3:7).

When the head of the household believed, everyone in his household was to be set apart to God. The proselyte was authorized and indeed obligated to bring his entire household into covenant with God because of his faith alone. In the Old Testament, the heathen proselyte and his household were considered the true seed of Abraham by faith (cf. Gen. 17:12–13; Ex. 12:48; Deut. 23:8). Gentiles became part of Abraham's seed by faith, although not in the numbers that they would in the new covenant era.[17]

God's Redemptive Promises to Parents

Parents know that the most precious thing that God has given them is their children. We love them, nurture them, instruct them, and, if necessary, would lay down our lives for them. Our greatest desire is to see them savingly know the Lord. Our heavenly Father appreciates the affection that we have for our families and has therefore made special redemptive provisions for the children and households of his people. John Calvin wrote about this fatherly love of God, "Let us accept as incontrovertible that God is so good and generous to his own as to be pleased, for their sake, also to count among his people the children whom they have begotten."[18]

Besides giving children to parents, God gave parents to children to represent their interests while they are minors. In this mutual relationship, both parents and children are blessed within the context of God's covenant. Charles Hodge observed,

> In the sight of God parents and children are one. The former are the authorized representatives of the latter; they act for them; they contract obligations in their name. In all cases, therefore, where parents enter into covenant with God, they bring their children with them. . . . It is vain to say that children cannot make contracts or take an oath. Their parents can act for them; and not only bring them under obligation, but secure for them the benefits of the covenants into which they vicariously enter. If a man joined the commonwealth of Israel he secured for his children the benefits of the theocracy, unless they willingly renounced them. And so when a believer adopts the covenant of grace, he brings his children within that covenant, in the sense that God promises to give them, in his own good time, all the benefits of redemption, provided they do not willingly renounce their baptismal engagements.[19]

Since God has purposed to redeem entire households, we would expect to find redemptive promises made to the heads of those households. The Bible is full of these promises. Such covenant promises are set within the context of God's everlasting commitment to his people. We are not left in the dark about God's intentions for our households.

One primary means of evangelism and kingdom expansion is the godly household. The Lord has purposed to use godly parents to beget a godly seed, which will go forth and establish new households to his glory. This purpose was expressed when God covenanted with Abraham and his children. In Genesis 18:19, the Lord details one of Abraham's primary duties: "For I have chosen him, in order that he may command his children and his household after him to keep the way of the LORD by doing righteousness and justice; in order that the LORD may bring upon Abraham what He has spoken about him."

The Lord repeatedly proclaims his intention to bless or curse successive generations on the basis of the faithfulness of parents. For example:

> You shall not worship them or serve them [idols]; for I, the LORD your God, am a jealous God, visiting the iniquity of the fathers on the children, on the third and fourth generations of those who hate Me, but showing lovingkindness to thousands, to those who love Me and keep My commandments. (Ex. 20:5–6)

> Know therefore that the LORD your God, He is God, the faithful God, who keeps His covenant and His lovingkindness to a thousandth generation with those who love Him and keep His commandments. (Deut. 7:9)[20]

> But the lovingkindness of the LORD is from everlasting to everlasting on those who fear Him, and His righteousness to children's children, to those who keep His covenant, and who remember His precepts to do them. (Ps. 103:17–18)

The Bible directs parents to teach God's words "diligently to your sons" (Deut. 6:7). With regard to God's laws, parents must "make them known to your sons and grandsons" (Deut. 4:9). David recorded the necessity and blessing of godly parental instruction (Ps. 78:4–6).

> We will not conceal them from their children, but tell to the generation to come the praises of the LORD, and His strength and His wondrous works that He has done. For He established a testimony in Jacob, and appointed a law in Israel, which He commanded our

fathers, that they should teach them to their children;
that the generation to come might know, even the children yet to be born, that they may arise and tell them
to their children.

Fathers are to bring up their children in "the discipline
and instruction of the Lord" (Eph. 6:4). The promise that God
attaches to all these duties of parental instruction is found in
Proverbs 22:6: "Train up a child in the way he should go, even
when he is old he will not depart from it." When parents faithfully instruct their children, they may expect that God will faithfully bring them to saving faith. Peter assured those parents
entering the new covenant that the promise was still for their
children (Acts 2:39). Even the Old Testament prophecies about
the coming new covenant reveal God's intentions for the children of believers. We read in Ezekiel 37:24–27 about the expected new covenant and the reign of Christ,

> And My servant David will be king over them, and they
> will all have one shepherd; and they will walk in My
> ordinances, and keep My statutes, and observe them.
> And they shall live on the land that I gave to Jacob My
> servant, in which your fathers lived; and they will live
> on it, *they, and their sons, and their son's sons, forever;* and
> David My servant shall be their prince forever. And I
> will make a covenant of peace with them; it will be an
> everlasting covenant with them. And I will place them
> and multiply them, and will set My sanctuary in their
> midst forever. My dwelling place also will be with them;
> and I will be their God, and they will be My people.

As the Lord promises a future Redeemer in Isaiah 59:20–
21, he also makes a promise to parents about their children's
place in his new covenant.

> "And a Redeemer will come to Zion, and to those who
> turn from transgression in Jacob," declares the Lord.

"And as for Me, this is My covenant with them," says the LORD: "My Spirit which is upon you, and My words which I have put in your mouth, shall not depart from your mouth, nor from the mouth of your offspring, nor from the mouth of your offspring's offspring," says the LORD, "from now and forever."

Parents of all generations have enjoyed these promises of God to redeem their children and their children's children. God has been pleased to embrace the households of his people in the covenant of grace from the beginning until now. What a delight it is to know that we may stand fully and securely on the promises of our covenant-keeping God and, by his grace, expect the fulfillment of those promises in our children and our children's children.

Children of Believers Set Apart

As the gospel spread for the first time to pagan cultures, the cohesion of the family was challenged as individual members of pagan families were converted to the faith. This is the situation Paul addresses in 1 Corinthians 7. He says that unbelieving spouses are sanctified and the children of believers are made holy by the believer (v. 14). But how could this be, if they were not covenantally set apart by God and put in a special or privileged category of humanity?

The answer is that the children of believers, while not automatically the recipients of saving grace, do come under the covenant of grace and thereby occupy a privileged position before God. They are set apart (i.e., "made holy") for a special redemptive purpose. Even in households where there is only one believing parent, the children occupy a distinctively privileged or consecrated position before the Lord: "For the unbelieving husband is sanctified through his wife, and the unbelieving wife is sanctified through her believing husband; for otherwise your children are unclean, but now they are holy" (v. 14).

How is it that the children of believers are called "holy" (i.e., "set apart")? What are they set apart from, and what are they set apart to? We know that this cannot mean that they are regenerate, for the unbelieving spouse is considered sanctified also. It is their being a member of the household of a believer that sanctifies or sets them apart. *They are set apart from the world and consecrated to God by virtue of their membership in a covenant household.* Greg Bahnsen elaborates on this point.

> Notice this further point. As a passing reinforcement of his explanation about covenantal consecration of the unbelieving spouse, Paul adds one more, short remark without elaboration (indicating that he expected his audience to understand the concept already). This is something which is just taken for granted in terms of New Testament theology. What he says at the end of verse 14 is this: "otherwise your children would be unclean, but now are they holy." That is, the children of even one believer are, in virtue of that family affiliation, viewed in a special way by God. They are not categorized with the world, even though they are as yet unbelievers. They are viewed—just as we have seen that the church as a whole is viewed—as "clean" and as "holy." Children of believers are not seen as part of the common world of unbelief and spiritual defilement, despite their need to come to conversion and confess faith in Christ the Savior. They are already "set apart" from the world and in a special, consecrated relationship to the Lord of the covenant because of their believing parent(s). They are deemed by God part of the covenant community on earth, the church—those whom Christ has made "holy, cleansing" them through the washing of water in the sphere of the word (cf. Eph. 5:26).[21]

These "holy, cleansed" children must receive the cleansing sign of baptism to mark them off from the "unholy" or defiled children of unbelievers, just as circumcision performed this task in the Old Testament. Even as the tabernacle and its utensils were sprinkled with blood for cleansing and consecration (Heb. 9:21–22), so too must the believer's children receive the cleansing of baptism, which sets them apart for God.

Jesus and the Little Children

When Jesus blessed the little children who were brought to him, no doubt by their believing parents, he taught that anyone who would enter the kingdom of God had to become like a child.[22] While aimed at adults, this teaching applied also to children, for they were already like children! The children brought to him certainly included infants.[23] The teaching of the Lord is that the kingdom belongs to such infants. He does not say "to those who resemble infants, but are not infants." It was real, not figurative children whom the disciples hindered from coming. And it was real children of whom Jesus said, "The kingdom belongs to such as these."[24]

The parents who brought these infant children to Jesus were certainly faithful to the covenant and recognized Jesus as the promised Messiah. This was a real blessing that they sought, and it was a real blessing that was conferred on them by Jesus. Jesus' invitation was no public relations ploy; it was an action of substance. As believing parents were members of the visible church, so too were their children. If the root is holy, so are the branches. These children of believers were received by Christ and blessed by him.

What Does This Have to Do with Infant Baptism?

Since the households of God's people included their children in the covenant of grace for such a long time—from the beginning of time—it seems fantastic to imagine that they would be excluded from the covenant of grace without notice in the pages of Scripture. Covenantal birth was highly prized among the Hebrews (cf. Matt. 3:9; John 8:33). For a Jew to be cut off from among his people was incredibly shameful and a dreaded disgrace. The Jews considered an uncircumcised man to be like a dog—unclean and loathsome. How could this privilege have been canceled without at least some mention of it in the Bible?[25]

The biblical idea of the household as a covenantal unit is a dominant feature of God's redemptive plan and remains intact in the New Testament. The head of the believing household has a duty to obligate his entire household to the service of God. We do not have the prerogative to exclude persons (including our children) from covenant privileges that God has always allowed. Nor may we withhold the sign and seal of covenant membership (baptism), which sets covenant members apart from the common pagan. We must say today, as did Joshua, "As for me and my house, we will serve the Lord."

NOTES

1. Alexander Carson, *Baptism: Its Mode and Subjects* (1853; reprint, Grand Rapids: Kregel, 1981), 181–82.
2. It should be noted that "servants" in the Scriptures were much more than employees. They were slaves who were cleary under the household authority.
3. A. H. Strong, *Systematic Theology* (Chicago: Judson, 1953), 955.
4. Allen C. Guelzo, *Who Should Be Baptized? A Case for the Baptism of Infants* (Philadelphia: Reformed Episcopal Publication Society, 1985), 18–19.
5. Ibid. For similar situations, see Matt. 9:18–19, 23–26; 17:14–18; Luke 7:11–17; John 4:46–54.
6. A major ideological shift began during the Renaissance. People began to be seen less as part of the community and more as individuals who stood apart from the corporate body. Allen Guelzo (*Who Should Be Baptized?*, 16) says, "It is probably no accident that the first appearance in church history [of those who practice believers' baptism only] occurs in the early 1500's—in other words, they appear at exactly the same time the Renaissance was exalting the individual and creating a philosophy of man-centered individualism of which we are all the heirs. This also explains the overwhelming popularity of Baptist churches in

America, for what else is America, culturally speaking, but the land of the supreme individual—of the loner who goes off on his own, carves out his own private frontier empire, farms and protects it by his own hand, and makes, 'Mind your own business' his unofficial creed? Do we wonder, with this being so much a part of our natural culture, that the Baptist, with his parallel stress on individualism in spiritual things should bulk so large on our horizon?"

7. Ibid., 13–14.
8. A. A. Hodge, *Evangelical Theology* (1890; reprint, Carlisle, Pa.: Banner of Truth, 1990), 178.
9. Robert L. Dabney, *Lectures in Systematic Theology* (1878; reprint, Grand Rapids: Zondervan, 1975), 783–84.
10. Kenneth L. Gentry, *The Greatness of the Great Commission* (Tyler, Tex.: Institute for Christian Economics, 1990), 87. This book explains the covenantal structure of the Great Commission and the fact that its focus cannot be limited to individuals.
11. Richard P. Flinn, "Baptism, Redemptive History, and Eschatology: Parameters of Debate," in *The Failure of the American Baptist Culture,* ed. James B. Jordan, Christianity and Civilization, no. 1 (Tyler, Tex.: Geneva Divinity School, 1982), 146–47.
12. Dabney, *Lectures in Systematic Theology,* 783–84.
13. William Cunningham, *Historical Theology* (1862; reprint, Carlisle, Pa.: Banner of Truth, 1979), 2:149.
14. John Owen, *The Works of John Owen* (1850–53; reprint, Carlisle, Pa.: Banner of Truth, 1981), 16:258–59.
15. Ibid., 259.
16. Cf. John 4:53; Acts 10:2; 16:14, 31–34, 40; 18:8; 1 Cor. 1:16; 16:15–19; 2 Tim. 4:19.
17. Dabney, *Lectures in Systematic Theology,* 782.
18. John Calvin, *Institutes of the Christian Religion,* ed. John T. McNeill (Philadelphia: Westminster Press, 1960), 2:1338.
19. Charles Hodge, *Systematic Theology* (Grand Rapids: Eerdmans, 1991), 3:555.
20. Cf. Ex. 34:7; Num. 14:18; Deut. 5:9.
21. Greg L. Bahnsen, "Infant Baptism," *The Counsel of Chalcedon* 15, no. 2 (April 1993); 15, no. 3 (May 1993); 15, no. 4 (June 1993). These articles explore further the idea of "holy" or "consecrated children," and are very helpful in that they show the reason why the children of believers are to be baptized. I would also recom-

mend Dr. Bahnsen's three tapes on "Biblical Baptism" (#TSB2), as well as his sixteen-tape series on covenant theology (#TSC2). All of these materials are available from Covenant Tape Ministry (1-800-553-3938).

22. Matt. 18:1–6, 14; 19:13–15; Mark 9:36–37; 10:13–16; Luke 18:15–17.

23. The Greek word used to describe the children brought to Jesus in Luke 18:15 is *brephe*, meaning "infants" or "nursing babes." Cf. also Luke 2:12, 16; Acts 7:19; 1 Peter 2:2, where the same word describes infants.

24. In Luke 18:16 the word translated "forbid them (not)" (*koluete*) is used pervasively in the New Testament for "(not) hindering" baptism! (e.g., Acts 8:36; 10:47; 11:17).

25. Dabney, *Lectures in Systematic Theology*, 786–87.

CHAPTER 8

Household Baptism: Your God Shall Be My God

JACK: I think I see what you mean about God dealing with people by way of covenants, but I still don't understand how a child, especially an infant, could be a part of God's covenant of grace. A small child can't even understand what it's all about, much less commit himself to keep such a covenant.

Jack was speaking with a friend of his, Paul Cowen, who was the pastor of Covenant Community Church. Paul had been talking with Jack from time to time about covenant theology, and he was hoping to see Jack come to understand the full counsel of God (expressed best in the Reformed faith).

JACK (continuing): Paul, can you explain how parents can bring their children into God's covenant without the children's personal commitment and profession of faith?

PAUL: Well, Jack, perhaps I can help by giving you an

illustration. Illustrations don't provide exact parallels, but they do sometimes help us get a handle on an idea. You're a citizen of the United States of America, aren't you?

JACK: Yes.

PAUL: How did you become a citizen?

JACK: My parents were citizens, and I became a citizen by virtue of the fact that I was their child.

PAUL: When you were an infant citizen of the United States, were you a full citizen with all the responsibilities and privileges of citizenship?

JACK: I think I was a full citizen, but I'm not sure about the other.

PAUL: You're right. You were a full citizen, who in principle had all the responsibilities and privileges of citizenship, but because of the limitations of your age, you neither could perform all the duties of citizenship nor had access to all the privileges. You didn't have the ability to work, pay taxes, or defend your country, and neither could you get a driver's license or vote. The reality of those things was still in the future.

JACK: So I really had no choice in the matter. I was a citizen whether I wanted to be or not.

PAUL: That's right. When you were too young to make such commitments, your parents brought you into the citizenship and protection of the state. However, as you grew older, you should have been taught by your parents just what your duties and privileges were as a citizen. For example, they probably taught you about many of the laws of the land and your obligation to be a law-abiding citizen. They also probably told you of the benefits of being an American.

JACK: You're right, they did both of those things.

PAUL: Then, as you grew older, you had the opportunity to either confirm or renounce your citizenship. You could have done this in a couple of ways. First, you could have verbally confirmed or professed your commitment to the country by saying the Pledge of Allegiance, or you could have declared that you no longer wanted to be a citizen of the U.S. and sought citizenship elsewhere. Second, you could have confirmed or renounced your citizenship by your behavior. By being a law-abiding citizen, you have demonstrated your commitment to live under the terms of citizenship. If you become a law breaker, the state will respond by removing some of the privileges of citizenship (e.g., by putting you in prison) or, if the crime is serious enough, it may even remove you from the citizenry by execution.

JACK: I see. I came under the protection and blessing of the United States by being born into a family of U.S. citizens, but as I grew older I had to either embrace and own that citizenship myself or else reject it and be rejected.

PAUL: That's right. One obligation of citizenship is that, as you are able, you must profess commitment to that citizenship verbally and though your conduct. Failure to do so could result in a loss of the benefits of citizenship.

JACK: So, children born into the households of believers come under the protection of God's covenant of grace?

PAUL: You've got it. And their parents are obligated to instruct them about the duties and privileges of covenant membership. One of the primary duties of remaining in that covenant is that the children, as they grow old enough to understand, must repent of their sins and by faith profess Christ as their Lord and Savior. Failure to embrace Jesus Christ would restrict access to many covenant privileges and would eventually lead to being excluded from the covenant community and ultimately result in being eternally separated from God.

JACK: This helps a great deal. I'll have to think about it for a while. I've got to go now, but I'll see you next Thursday, Paul.

PAUL: I enjoyed our conversation and I'll look forward to next week.

Household Baptisms

We turn now to the much-disputed topic of the household baptisms found in the New Testament. There is no explicit mention of there being any infants in the households that were baptized. Neither are we told that there were no infants in these households. We are only informed that households, as households, were baptized. Given the biblical understanding of what a household comprised, we may safely conclude that *if* there were any infants present in these households, they were most certainly baptized. Moreover, the case for infant baptism does not hinge on the presence of infants in these households.

Our understanding of these passages about household baptisms depends on whether we come to them with a covenantal (Reformed) or a dispensational (baptistic) point of view. From the covenantal perspective, these texts are in full support of, and consistent with, the paedobaptist view. Those who hold the dispensational view likewise believe that they can harmonize these texts with their overall system. J. A. Alexander, in his commentary on Acts, wrote,

> The whole dispute, however, rests on grounds entirely independent of these cases, and every reader will interpret these according to his views of those. He who believes in the perpetuity of the patriarchal covenant, with a change in the accompanying seal, will need no proof that children were baptized with their parents upon such occasions; whereas, he whose very definition of the ordinance excludes children, will of course deny their actual reception of it in all given cases.[1]

Keeping in mind the points already set forth in this book—i.e., continuity of the covenants, continuity of the church, continuity of the covenant signs, and continuity of the covenant household—let us examine the record of household baptisms.

The Acts of the Apostles records a period of history that extends from about A.D. 30 to A.D. 63. Thousands of people during this period were baptized, but only a few are specifically mentioned by name: the Ethiopian eunuch, Simon Magus, Saul of Tarsus, Cornelius, Lydia, the Philippian jailer, and Crispus of Corinth. Altogether, in the book of Acts, seven specific accounts of baptism are recorded. In 1 Corinthians, the baptisms of Gaius and Stephanas are also mentioned. That makes a total of nine people in the New Testament who are mentioned by name as having been baptized.

Now since families then tended to be large, these households, taken together, probably included persons of all ages. John P. Sartelle comments,

> Some have said we cannot prove there were children in those households. However, to assume that these homes, along with the other households baptized in the Mediterranean area, had no children is a presumption bordering on prejudice. Can we say that the household baptisms mentioned were the only ones and that in every case the converts were childless and that their servants were childless?[2]

Nevertheless, our immediate concern is not whether there were infants in these households, since the Reformed paedobaptist argument does not rest on the presence of infants in baptized households. There is a larger issue than infant baptism in view here, and that is the baptism of all household members (not just infants) by virtue of the faith of household heads. The individuals within households were baptized not because they necessarily believed (though some may well have) but rather, *because they were members of the households of believers.*

Of the nine persons mentioned as having been baptized, two probably did not have immediate families—Saul and the Ethiopian eunuch. We are not informed about any family of two others, Simon Magus and Gaius. In the remaining five cases, the entire household was baptized.[3] We may conclude, then, that *in every case where the apostles administered baptism to the known head of a family, they also administered it to his entire household.* The church father Origen apparently was not mistaken when he said that the church had received the tradition of infant baptism from the apostles.[4]

The Philippian Jailer and His Household

The account of the baptism of the Philippian jailer and his household is found in Acts 16:30–34. The text does not tell of anyone believing except the jailer himself. Although it is possible that some others in his household did believe, the text does not say so, any more than it says whether there were infants present in the household.

We are told that the jailer believed and that he and his household were baptized. The only reason actually given for the other household members' being baptized was that they were members of the believing jailer's household. In fact, before his household had ever been spoken to, Paul and Silas assured the jailer that salvation (i.e., redemption) would come to his entire household because of his belief in the Lord Jesus: "He said, 'Sirs, what must I do to be saved?' And they said, 'Believe in the Lord Jesus, and you shall be saved, you and your household'" (Acts 16:30–31).

This statement about the jailer's household was made before anything was said to the other members of his household. Perhaps Paul and Silas were prophesying about the individual members of the jailer's household—but that seems implausible. More likely, Paul and Silas were referring to the practice of including whole households in the covenant of grace. They expected that if the jailer professed faith in Christ, then his entire household would be baptized and brought into the redemptive covenant because of the believing head of the household.

Some argue that the household of the jailer was made up only of believing adults, because of the words "having believed in God with his whole household" in Acts 16:34. However, the original is not very accurately expressed by this English translation. An accurate translation from the Greek would be either "and rejoiced with all his house, he having believed in God" or "having believed in God, he rejoiced with all his house." Most Baptist scholars agree on this point, but they argue that since the jailer's household rejoiced with him, they must have all been adults. However, we often find rejoicing children in the Bible. The little children in the temple rejoiced and said, "Hosanna to the Son of David," and Jesus described the situation by saying, "Have you never read, 'Out of the mouth of infants and nursing babes Thou hast prepared praise for Thyself'?" (Matt. 21:15–16). We read in Deuteronomy 14:26, "You shall eat in the presence of the LORD your God and rejoice, you and your household."

The fact that Paul and Silas "spoke the word of the Lord to him together with all who were in his house" (Acts 16:32) does not imply that there were no infants or small children present. Surely every pastor has spoken to the "whole congregation" and had infants and small children present. In Joshua 8:35 we are told, "There was not a word of all that Moses had commanded which Joshua did not read before all the assembly of Israel with the women and the little ones and the strangers who were living among them."

This account of a household baptism fits well with the covenantal understanding of biblical households and the inclusion of all the members of the family in the redemptive purposes of God.

The Household of Cornelius

Cornelius was a Gentile, a God-fearer, who was well acquainted with Jewish practices. To argue that as a Gentile he would not have expected his children to be included in baptism overlooks two important points. First, the Gentiles in the Roman Empire also held to a strong concept of the household, perhaps even stronger than the Jews in some aspects. These Gentiles did not think in individualistic terms.[5] Second, Cornelius was aware of the Jewish practice of including infants in the covenant.

Cornelius is described in Acts 10:2 as "a devout man, and one who feared God with all his household." Some argue from this that only adults were present in the house of Cornelius. Yet, it is not unusual for this sort of language to be applied to families that contain small children. We might refer to a family as a "God-fearing family," a "godly family," or a "Christian family," even though every individual in that family may not have professed personal faith. Nor would it be unusual for small children to have the fear of God in some degree. Joshua speaks for his family when he says, "As for me and my house, we will serve the LORD" (Josh. 24:15), and we would not think it inappropriate for such a statement to be made by a father on behalf of all those in his household, including infants.

Acts 10:44 says, "The Holy Spirit fell upon all those who were listening to the message." This does not prove that only adults were present in the house of Cornelius. It is not uncommon to use language such as "The whole audience was moved" to describe such a situation. By such language we do not necessarily exclude infants. It is also clear from the text that many people, other than his family, were assembled at the house of Cornelius and were included in the description of the events taking place (Acts 10:24, 27).

The Household of Lydia

Some Baptists argue that all in Lydia's household were adult believers inasmuch as the apostles "entered the house of Lydia, and when they saw the brethren, they encouraged them and departed" (Acts 16:40). According to this reasoning, these "brethren," being adult believers, were all those who made up Lydia's household. But is it not more reasonable to understand that a group of believers from Philippi gathered at Lydia's house to say farewell to Paul and Silas?

Luke describes Lydia's conversion and baptism in Acts 16:14–15.

> A certain woman named Lydia, from the city of Thyatira, a seller of purple fabrics, a worshiper of God, was listening; and the Lord opened her heart to respond to the things spoken by Paul. And when she and her household had been baptized, she urged us, saying, "If

you have judged me to be faithful to the Lord, come into my house and stay." And she prevailed upon us.

Luke specifically indicates that Lydia responded to Paul. He tells us nothing about her family until he says that "she and her household" were baptized. The only conclusion we can draw about the baptism of the other members of Lydia's household is that they were baptized because they were members of the household of the believer Lydia. Both the Baptist and the Reformed paedobaptist must bring their presuppositions to bear upon this and other household baptism texts. J. A. Alexander observed,

> Both parties reason in a circle from foregone conclusions; one contending that as infants are incapable of faith, there either were none, or they were excluded from the ordinance; the other, that as households include children, we have no right to except them from the general statement. The real strength of the latter argument lies not in any one case, but in the repeated mention of whole houses as baptized.[6]

The Household of Crispus

Acts 18:8 says, "And Crispus, the leader of the synagogue, believed in the Lord with all his household, and many of the Corinthians when they heard were believing and being baptized." On the surface, this passage seems to indicate that not only Crispus, but also every member of his household, was a believer. This is indeed entirely possible. Nevertheless, since Crispus was the leader of the synagogue, his entire household, including his children, would have belonged to the synagogue. It seems likely, then, that Crispus, as the head of his house, would have brought his entire family for household baptism.

Moreover, we must keep in mind that missionaries have seen entire families or tribes make professions of faith because the head of the family or tribe did so. We should expect that a first-century Jewish family would similarly have followed the lead of its covenantal head. This text should be interpreted in accordance with the Jewish culture of the times, not the individualistic assumptions of our own culture. Vern Poythress observes, "In modern times, there are incidents where the tribal chief announces that 'we are becoming Christians,' and the whole tribe asks to be baptized. Individualistic Americans are not used to this type of procedure, but it is not rare or absurd."[7]

The New Testament culture arose from the Old Testament culture, and therefore it is not surprising to find whole households believing because the head of the household believes. Consider the similarly covenantal thinking in what Ruth says to Naomi in Ruth 1:16–17:

> Do not urge me to leave you or turn back from following you; for where you go, I will go, and where you lodge, I will lodge. Your people shall be my people, and your God, my God. Where you die, I will die, and there I will be buried. Thus may the LORD do to me, and worse, if anything but death parts you and me.

The Household of Stephanas

The account of the baptism of the household of Stephanas is found in 1 Corinthians 1:14–16, where Paul says, "I thank God that I baptized none of you except Crispus and Gaius, that no man should say you were baptized in my name. Now I did baptize also the household of Stephanas; beyond that, I do not know whether I baptized any other."

Crispus has already been mentioned in Acts, and we do not know whether Gaius had any immediate family. We are further told in 1 Corinthians 16:15 that the household of Stephanas was "the first fruits of Achaia." In none of this is there any contradiction of the covenantal understanding of household baptism. The one clear fact emerging from these texts is that whenever the head of a family was baptized, so was his or her entire household. The Bible does not tell us that the household was baptized because each member of it believed and professed personal faith (although some may indeed have believed). The reason given in Scripture for the baptism of household members is that they were members of the household.

Households or Individuals?

The individualism that sprang forth from the Renaissance has caused us to lose sight of the biblical concept of the family as a covenantal unit. It seems odd to many that God could have any redemptive concerns beyond the salvation of individual souls. Any other interest would not be "fair." Yet God not only elects individuals unconditionally but also works redemptively through households. Allen Guelzo has written about this cultural influence of Renaissance individualism,

> I suspect our difficulty in answering the question [of who should be baptized] stems less from a lack of biblical evidence and more from an inability to recognize that evidence when we see it, chiefly because our ways of thinking have changed so drastically from the ways of thinking natural to the authors of the New Testament, something which applies especially to the way we think about the family. Our difficulty in understanding the New Testament's answer to this question is not one of theology, but history, and only if we can get this mental blockage out of our way, then the answer to the question, "who are the proper subjects of baptism?" will, in large measure, take care of itself.[8]

Consequently, if God continues to deal with us as families in his covenant, then we need to give some very serious consideration to what we are doing if we leave our children unbaptized. We are not leaving them free to exercise their own free choice in a democratic uni-

verse. Instead, we are forcing them to break God's covenant; we are depriving them of what they have a legitimate right to; and we are making them to be
covenant-breakers in the eyes of God.[9]

What Does This Have to Do with Infant Baptism?

It is difficult to think in patterns that are foreign to our own
culture. Yet, we must interpret the Bible from the perspective
of those who first heard its words. The first-century culture
was a corporate society that thought in terms of whole families
as units. It was the exception to the rule for some members of
a household to reject the faith of its head.

I am not denying the necessity of individual, personal faithfulness to the covenant. However, the requirement of individual faithfulness is not a novelty introduced in the New
Testament. Inclusion in the covenant has never automatically
conferred personal salvation on any individual. All men must
repent and believe. This was just as true in the Old Testament
as it is in the New. The entire chapter of Ezekiel 18 emphasizes
the individual's responsibility to obey God and live—father and
son alike. "Behold, all souls are Mine; the soul of the father as
well as the soul of the son is Mine. The soul who sins will die"
(v. 4).

All family members come under the redemptive umbrella
of the covenant household. They are set apart, are instructed
in the faith, and receive many covenant privileges. They are
likewise obligated to repent of their sins, believe on Jesus Christ,
and faithfully follow him in obedience. As Ben House comments, "It's not like we can hide under our mother's theological skirts. We will all give an individual account of ourselves
before God."[10]

Under the baptistic scheme, household baptisms are an
anomaly—an unusual occurrence for an individualistic gospel. From the covenantal point of view, however, household
baptisms would be routine and ordinary. An examination of
the New Testament record demonstrates that household bap-

tisms were indeed the rule, not the exception. In every case where the head of a household believed, that household head and his or her entire household were baptized. It is the covenantal perspective that provides a clear and simple explanation for the widespread practice of household baptism in the apostolic church.

NOTES

1. J. A. Alexander, *Acts* (1857; reprint, Carlisle, Pa.: Banner of Truth, 1980), 2:113.
2. John P. Sartelle, *Infant Baptism: What Christian Parents Should Know* (Phillipsburg, N.J.: Presbyterian and Reformed, 1985), 8.
3. See also John 4:46–53, a possible sixth case of household baptism. A royal official comes to Jesus in Galilee, representing his sick son in Capernaum. On the basis of the father's belief in the words of Jesus, the son is healed. While we are not specifically told that the household was baptized, we are told that the father believed with his whole household, thus following the pattern.
4. Ashbel G. Fairchild, *Scripture Baptism, Its Mode and Subjects* (Philadelphia: Presbyterian Board of Publication, 1858), 141, 143–44. Origen's parents had him baptized as an infant in c. 185, less than one hundred years after the apostles.
5. Carle C. Zimmerman and Lucius F. Cervantes, *Marriage and the Family* (Chicago: Henry Regnery, 1956), 457–59. These authors point out that the predominant form of the family structure in ancient Roman civilization, beginning with the founding of Rome in 735 B.C., can be summarized by the phrase *patria potestas* or "father-power." "This 'paternal prerogative' meant that the head *male* in the family (whether with or without the agreement and counsel of the rest of the family . . .) had the power of life and death not only over his wife but his children and any other members of his patriarchal domain. As the ruler of the paternal manse the male who had the paternal right had the rights of the chief executive, legislator, and judge; this latter office included the power of life and death of the constituent members under his jurisdiction. . . . A woman never properly had her own religion; she was always considered as a part of her husband's or father's or son's religion." Fustel de Coulanges identifies the source of this "father-power": "The authority of the father or husband, far

from having been a first cause, was itself an effect; it was DE-
RIVED FROM RELIGION, AND WAS ESTABLISHED BY
RELIGION. . . . The members of the ancient family were united
by something more powerful than birth, affection, or physical
strength; this was the religion of the sacred fire, and of dead
ancestors. This caused the family to form a single body, both in
this life and the next. The ancient family was a religious rather
than a natural association . . . the heir who refused to adopt the
worship of the family had no right to succession."

6. Alexander, *Acts*, 2:113.
7. Letter from Vern S. Poythress to the author, March 3, 1993.
8. Allen C. Guelzo, *Who Should Be Baptized? A Case for the Baptism of Infants* (Philadelphia: Reformed Episcopal Publication Society, 1985), 6–7.
9. Ibid., 20–21.
10. J. Ben House, Bible study notes on Neh. 8 (Texarkana, Ark., 1993).

CHAPTER 9

Close to Home: Weighing the Case for Infant Baptism

STEVE AND JANE, having read Randy's book, go to his house to discuss it. The three of them sit down in Randy's living room and pursue a few remaining matters.

STEVE: Randy, your book was really helpful to Jane and me. We're not sure exactly where we stand ourselves, but we can see a little better where you're coming from. We do still have some unanswered questions.

RANDY: I appreciate your taking the time to read the book and your being fair-minded about it. I know you both realize that no single book can deal with every question pertaining to this subject. I do hope you will read others and continue to seek understanding in the matter.

JANE: It's hard to look at something from a totally different perspective than what you're used to. I've always been a Baptist and just thought infant baptism was crazy. But I must

153

admit, I've wondered for a long time how so many Reformed Christians, with their firm commitment to the Bible, could hold to the doctrine of infant baptism. I guess I never really looked into it before.

RANDY: I can appreciate what you're saying, since that pretty much describes my own background. I think we're all fairly good at knowing what we believe, but we're often not so good at knowing why.

STEVE: I'm still not sure what I believe on baptism, but you sure have me studying my Bible. At least I have a greater appreciation for my Reformed paedobaptist brethren and their commitment to Scripture as their only authority. But I agree with Jane. It's not only hard to change one's position, it's even hard to consider another position.

RANDY: I understand. That's because presuppositional changes are always the hardest to make. We're not just talking about changing your view of one particular doctrine out there all by itself. We're talking about a different way of looking at the Scriptures—seeing the Old and New Testaments as one unified book. The Baptists and the Reformed paedobaptists have different starting points, and this is always the first issue that must be settled.

JANE: Yeah, the thing I hadn't given much thought to was the family context of the Bible, especially in the New Testament. The household really was the basic social unit. It's easy just to assume that everyone has always thought and functioned the way we do; and it's hard not to read your own cultural biases into whatever you're studying.

RANDY: You're not kidding. We have to fight against the strong tendency to see things only one way—our way.

STEVE: I have to be honest with you, Randy; one of the biggest problems I'm having is that I just don't want to be a paedobaptist—I've been comfortable being a Baptist. Changing my view on baptism would create a lot of disruptions in my life.

RANDY: I sure can relate to that. I've had more than a few tense moments myself as I've wrestled with this issue. I don't like change, and I love stability and security. There have been many moments during my study of this topic when I wished I could find some way to set it aside. But truth and faithfulness to God must come before personal security. Jesus didn't "go along to get along," and neither can we.

STEVE: I know, it's just such a struggle. At times I wonder what difference it all makes anyway whether we baptize infants.

RANDY: I've wondered that, too, but I'll have to give the Reformed paedobaptist answer. We have lost sight of corporate realities and the importance and value of symbolic measures. The Bible says that the inclusion of the children of believers is very important: "Permit the children to come to Me." We baptize the children of believers because the Bible tells us to—"for the kingdom of God belongs to such as these." We have no confirmation of the truth of God's promise if the sign and seal of that promise is denied. God's assurance to believers that he is indeed a God to their children, in addition to themselves, is that he has granted the sign and seal of the covenant of grace to them and their children. If children are not baptized, then the promise made to the children of believers is not confirmed by Christ.

JANE: Randy, before you gave me your book, you overheard me asking, "How could anyone believe in baptizing babies?" I have to confess that at the time I wasn't really looking for an answer. I was mad at you for rocking the boat.

RANDY: Well, you may not accept the covenantal position yourself, but can you see now why others might?

JANE: I think I can, but it might be helpful if you gave me a quick summary of your position again—kind of a snapshot without all the details.

RANDY: Well, there were five main points.

JANE: Let me jot them down.

STEVE: Good idea. I'd like to review them myself.

RANDY: The most important point was the first one, about our interpretive principle. Sometimes you will hear people talk about the "general tenor" of the New Testament, or they will

say that when they first read the Bible as new Christians, infant baptism didn't exactly jump off the page at them. So they
conclude that such doctrines must not be true. You'll even hear
some well-intentioned Christians demand "an explicit verse"
that teaches infant baptism. Thankfully, most believers recognize that good theology is not done by the "general tenor"
method (since none of us is without some bias), nor is it done
best by new Christians. And we don't determine all of our doctrines by "explicit verses"; otherwise, we wouldn't be Trinitar-
ians and we would forbid women to come to the Lord's Table.
We all hold many doctrines by biblical inference.

   Our interpretive starting point will determine how we
understand the Bible. Most people do not consistently apply
any interpretive principle, yet we should all strive for interpretive consistency. The Reformed or covenantal principle of interpretation holds that we must read the Bible as one book that
progressively reveals God's one redemptive purpose. We need
to assume continuity and unity in God's revelation. Unless God
himself has explicitly changed some aspect of his redemptive
dealings with his people, we should continue to follow what he
has already revealed. Because the children of believers were
always included in the covenant of grace in the Old Testament,
and God nowhere rescinds his command to include them in
the covenant of grace, we must assume that they are still to be
included under the new covenant and are to receive the covenant sign of baptism.

   The dispensational or baptistic principle of interpretation
sees the new covenant as a complete replacement of the older
covenants, and therefore holds that we must gain our understanding of baptism from the New Testament alone. Since there
is no explicit command in the New Testament to baptize infants, we must assume, on this view, that the children of believers are not to be included in the new covenant. The Old
Testament has no bearing on the subject of baptism—it is a
New Testament ordinance.

   Keep in mind that many believers try to stand somewhere
between these two interpretive principles (although they may

not realize it). For example, they may be covenantal in their view of the law and dispensational in their view of baptism. Or, they may be dispensational in their view of the law and covenantal in their view of baptism. We must strive for interpretive consistency. All the other arguments over infant baptism turn on this point.

JANE: So, you have to know where you're coming from in order to know whether you're heading in the right direction?

RANDY: That's right. Our interpretive principle, which sets our direction, has to be justified from the Bible. That is what I believe the next four points establish.

STEVE: Isn't the next point the continuity of the covenants?

RANDY: That's right. It's essential that we understand that God's only redemptive plan is what we call the "covenant of grace." This single covenant is revealed from the time of man's fall into sin until God accomplishes all of his redemptive purposes.

JANE: Did I understand you to say that there are other covenants that come under this one covenant of grace?

RANDY: Yes, down through redemptive history, God revealed more and more of his plan to save his people. He did this through particular covenants that he made with specific individuals and their families. God made covenants with Adam, Noah, Abraham, Moses, and David, culminating in the new covenant under Jesus. These covenants are related to each other in that they are all part of the covenant of grace. The new covenant did not dispense with the older covenants. Instead, it built upon their foundation and fulfilled their promises.

JANE: Your point here is that the children of believers were always included in the covenant of grace in the past, and there is no biblical reason why they should no longer be included in it.

RANDY: That's correct.

STEVE: And wasn't your third point about the church being identical in the Old and New Testaments?

RANDY: Well, I would want to qualify that a bit. The institution that we call the "church" underwent some significant changes during the New Testament era. God ordered the local church in new ways and provided more specific instruction for how it was to function. This was necessary to meet the new international challenges that God's people would face. Nevertheless, the church remained essentially the same as it had always been—that is, the people of God, set apart for his service. So, we could say that the people of God in the Old Testament and the people of God in the New Testament are identical in their essential nature. God included the infant children of believers in the membership of the Old Testament church, and there is no indication that he has changed the terms of membership for those who are to be considered "his people."

STEVE: Doesn't infant baptism carry the danger of producing a church of nominal or social Christians?

RANDY: Certainly it does, but I don't think the Baptists have avoided that danger, either. In other words, the problem of nominal church members plagues every church that is not faithful to perform all of its disciplining duties, whether they are paedobaptist or Baptist churches. When people fail to perform all their duties before God, then the danger of bad results is real. It's the duty of the church not only to include the infants of believers among its membership but also to instruct all of its members in the necessity of repentance and faith and their need of regeneration by the Holy Spirit. Preaching and instruction that causes all members to continually examine themselves to see if they are indeed in the faith is a primary responsibility of the church.

STEVE: What if some of these baptized children don't embrace the faith or prove to be ungodly in their conduct?

RANDY: Again, every local church faces the potential problem of having baptized members, regardless of their age when baptized, who never manifest the fruit of repentance. That's why, in addition to the formative discipline of instruction from the Word of God, the church must also perform its duty of corrective discipline from the Word, even to the point of excommunication.

JANE: In other words, the age at which people are baptized is not the real problem. It's the failure of churches to perform their other God-given duties that results in so many nominal church members.

RANDY: I think so.

JANE: Your fourth point, about the continuity of the covenant signs, circumcision and baptism, really made me rethink what I had always thought about them. I guess I really hadn't been taught that much about them, but just assumed I understood them.

RANDY: Yeah, well, when we know that two things are different in some ways, it's easy to assume that they are different in every way. The fact is that things can be, and often are, both different in some ways and alike in other ways. Circumcision and baptism are different in form—a bloody rite performed only on males compared with the application of water to both males and females. Yet, circumcision and baptism are alike in that they carry the same meaning. Both signs are the initiatory rites for those entering into the covenant of grace. They both are external signs of what should be true of God's people. Both indicate a putting away of the old sinful man and a putting on of the renewed man. They both are pictures of a repentant, cleansed heart—a seal of the righteousness that is by faith. So, while their outward form has changed, the essence of their meaning remains the same, and this is the most important part of the rite. The infant children of believers in the Old Testament were to receive the covenant sign and seal of justification by faith, and, likewise, the children of believers under the new covenant are to receive the covenant sign and seal.

STEVE: When I read the New Testament, I see baptism always connected to repentance and faith. How can infants repent and have faith?

RANDY: Steve, it's important to keep the context of the New Testament in mind when we read these verses. There the gospel is going to the Gentile or pagan nations for the first time. The first new converts to the faith will naturally be adults. Reformed paedobaptists agree that these adult converts must repent and believe before being baptized. Yet the Bible no-where excludes the children of these new converts from also receiving the covenant sign and seal, which places God's claim upon them and makes them heirs of the promise, even as the believer Abraham's children were.

JANE: So, you do believe in believers' baptism, but not only in believers' baptism?

RANDY: That's right, we believe that the verses Steve is referring to, concerning repentance and faith, apply to adult converts to the faith. It's just that we never see the children of those adult converts being excluded from the covenant of grace.

STEVE: That kind of leads to your fifth point, doesn't it?

RANDY: Yes, it does. God's redemptive concern for entire households is seen from cover to cover in the Bible. While by itself this doesn't deductively "prove" infant baptism, it cer-tainly goes a long way to inductively support the previous points I've made.

JANE: I have to agree that God has always shown a special interest in the children of his people. In fact, I've been puz-zled in the past when I read in the Bible about whole house-holds being blessed or cursed based upon the faith or conduct of the head of the household.

RANDY: I know what you mean, Jane. As parents, you and I know that our children benefit when we make good decisions, and they suffer when we don't. God has sovereignly given our children to us, and he has set them apart, as the children of believers, for special privilege. Baptism is the sign and seal that marks them out as those who are heirs to the promises made to the fathers.

STEVE: Are you saying that they automatically receive the promised blessing of salvation?

RANDY: Not at all! Every person, especially those who are covenantally obligated by baptism, must repent of their sins, believe on the Lord Jesus Christ, and profess him before oth-ers. That is the primary duty of everyone who enters the cov-enant of grace. Failure to follow after God from the heart will only lead to covenant curses.

STEVE: I guess I've thought for so long in terms of seeing individuals saved that it's hard for me to conceive of salvation in any other way.

RANDY: Well, let me emphasize my concern for the salvation of individual souls. God has always directed his electing love toward individual sinners. However, that's not all he has been concerned with. Society in general, and the family in particular, have likewise been the objects of his redemptive concern. So, it is not an either-or situation. God is concerned both about the salvation of the individual believer and about that of his household and society.

STEVE: Another thing that has bothered me is that I've been told that Baptists believe in "disciple baptism" but that paedobaptists don't.

RANDY: We have to be careful about how terms like that are used. What do you mean by "disciple baptism"?

STEVE: Well, I've always assumed that a disciple is someone who has decided to follow Jesus.

RANDY: More accurately, a disciple is a student, or one who learns. As believing parents, we make our infant children disciples from the time they're born, instructing them in many things concerning the Christian faith. Every time we teach them, and every time we bring them to church to be instructed, we are making them disciples or students.

STEVE: But all the children of the church don't grow up to be faithful Christians.

RANDY: Unfortunately, that's true, and neither do all the people who make professions of faith turn out to be faithful Christians.

STEVE: So, how can we really call them disciples?

RANDY: If I asked a school teacher how many students he had in his history class, what would he say?

STEVE: I suppose he would tell you the total number that were enrolled in the class.

RANDY: That's right. But suppose I asked that teacher about a student in his class named John, and the teacher replied, "Yes, John is in my class, but he's not a student." And suppose I asked that same teacher about another student in his class named Kimberly, and he replied, "Oh, now Kimberly is a student!" Are John and Kimberly both students?

STEVE: I see. You're using the word "student" in different ways and with different meanings.

RANDY: Yes, and likewise we may think of disciples in different ways. We may not be able to tell in kindergarten who is going to turn out to be a good or bad student, but in time it will become evident. In the meantime, they are all treated the same and taught the same material. So too, the children of believers are made into disciples or students and taught God's Word. In time, if parents and the church are faithful in their duties toward these children, most will become disciples indeed—true followers of Jesus Christ.

STEVE: So, Reformed paedobaptists do believe in "disciple baptism."

RANDY: Sure.

JANE: You know, another point you made that struck home was this notion of the Bible being sharply divided between Old and New Testaments. I have to confess that I've found myself thinking in terms of the God of the Old Testament and the God of the New Testament. Now, when I think about it, that seems absurd.

RANDY: Yeah, I don't think many of us are aware of just how much the subtle influence of dispensationalism has affected us. We are influenced without even being aware of it. Even our language reflects that influence when we speak of being New Testament Christians, as opposed to the more biblical idea of being believers who embrace the whole Bible as authoritative. Reformed or covenant theology does justice to the unity of God and the unity of the Bible.

STEVE: When I started studying the subject of baptism, I thought I could just study that topic by itself. I found out in a hurry that the issue was much bigger than a simple topical study. This is really about one's presuppositions, isn't it?

RANDY: I'm glad to hear you say that, Steve. Few people appreciate the fact that we must understand what our basic presuppositions are and then seek to apply them consistently. Covenant theology is a package deal. I can't hold to it when it suits me and then pick up dispensational presuppositions when they give me the results I want. All of our doctrinal understanding, not just the doctrine of baptism, is affected by the assumptions with which we start.

JANE: The hard part is being consistent.

STEVE: You've got to know what your presuppositions are before you can be consistent with them!

RANDY: You're both right. We have to keep laboring in God's Word so that we can grow in these areas of the Christian faith.

STEVE: Jane and I were talking before we came over here, and we were wondering what these changes in doctrine mean for our church. We're worried that it means we can't all stay together.

RANDY: You may be right. And I can't express to you how much that concern has occupied my mind, and just how many sleepless nights I've had over the past several months as a result. I love all of our church members—they're my family. You both know that the one thing our church has stressed over the years is the need to test everything by the Scriptures. That's what I have tried to do for myself on this issue.

JANE: But are you absolutely certain that you're right and that the Baptists are wrong?

RANDY: Jane, if there's one thing I have learned over the years as a Christian, it's that I can be wrong about a lot of things. We all agree that every person and every church has a mixture of truth and error. Do you know what your errors are?

JANE: I guess not. If I did, I'd change them.

RANDY: You're right; and therefore, we all need humility, regardless of our position on baptism. But let me make it clear to both of you that, after a great deal of study and consideration of both sides of this issue, I'm convinced in my mind and heart that covenant theology and infant baptism are true. I have a clear conscience before God in this matter.

JANE: Randy, when I started to read your book, I was pretty skeptical about how anyone could believe in infant baptism. But, I have to confess, you've given me a lot to think about.

STEVE: I don't know if you've convinced me yet, but I'm studying my Bible more than I have in a long time.

RANDY: That's all I could ever ask of anyone. This isn't a matter of choosing up sides and going to battle. I assume that every sincere Christian wants to know the truth and desires the will of God. I know that most of my Baptist brethren love the Lord and believe and practice what they do because they believe their view is biblical. I trust that they will grant me the same consideration. The truth can be known, but it may take a great deal of work in the Scriptures before we lay hold of it. Not all believers are going to come to the same understanding, and even if they do, it may not be at the same time. Jane, at least now you know the answer to your question, "How could anyone believe that?" Those of us who believe in household baptism do so because we believe that that is what the Bible teaches.

JANE: Thanks for your time, Randy. I have to be going now.

STEVE: Me too. Our visit has been very helpful. I've still got a lot of work to do.

RANDY: Let's pray before you go and ask God's blessing upon our lives.

The three friends join hands and Randy leads them in prayer, asking the Lord to assist them in their studies and calling upon him to bless their church as they consider the important issue of baptism.

ALL TRUTH, even when we fight against it at first, sets us free in the end. What at first we cannot see at all, we come to embrace and love. Suddenly, the beauty of its instruction is seen on every page of Scripture, and we wonder how we ever missed seeing it in the first place. Rather than being the monster I imagined, the doctrine of household baptism is now a comfort and a friend. The knowledge that God has set apart my family, including my beloved children, for special covenant blessings and promises is reassuring to me as a believer who labors to train them in the fear of the Lord. It is a comfort to know that the Lord has promised redemptive blessings to the household of believers who are faithful to his covenant; it is a comfort to know that we serve a covenant-keeping God. I once hated the doctrines of grace because I did not understand them and thought that they opposed evangelism and the kingdom of God. Now I love the doctrines of grace and know them to be the very gospel that advances God's kingdom. Infant baptism is a blessing to God's people, not an enemy.

I hope this short presentation of the Reformed paedobaptist position has been useful to you. With emotional issues, such as baptism, it is difficult for many of us to consider another position, and emotions often prove to be an obstacle to even understanding another position. I have struggled more with this issue than with any other I have ever faced, so I can sympathize with any of you who may also be wrestling with it. Keep laboring in the Scriptures to know the truth. For those of you who have been able to get beyond the emotions, I trust that you may now at least have a new appreciation for those of us who believe in infant baptism. We hold our position because we firmly and sincerely believe that this is what the Bible teaches.

I conclude with some remarks from a sermon on "Parental Responsibilities," by Robert L. Dabney in 1879:

> We observe some sincere Christians, whose minds are so swayed by the assertion that personal faith must be the invariable pre-requisite to baptism and admission to the church, that they seem incapable of ever entertaining the thought that the church membership of the children of believers may be reasonable and scriptural. The doctrine seems to them so great an anomaly that they cannot look dispassionately at the evidence for it. But to one who has weighed the truths set forth above,

the absence of that doctrine from God's dispensations would seem the strange anomaly. To him who has appreciated the parental relation as God represents it, the failure to include it within the circuit of the visible church, to sanctify its obligations and to seal its hopes with the sacramental badge, would appear the unaccountable thing. . . .

The instrumentalities of the family are chosen and ordained of God as the most efficient of all means of grace—more truly and efficaciously means of saving grace than all the other ordinances of the church. To family piety are given the best promises of the gospel, under the new, as well as under the old dispensation. How, then, should a wise God do otherwise than consecrate the Christian family, and ordain that the believing parents shall sanctify the children? Hence, the very foundation of all parental fidelity to children's souls is to be laid in the conscientious, solemn, and hearty adoption of the very duties and promises which God seals in the covenant of infant baptism. It is pleasing to think that many Christians who refuse the sacrament do, with a happy inconsistency, embrace the duties and seek the blessing. But God gives all his people the truths and promises, along with the edifying seal. Let us hold fast to both.[1]

NOTES

1. Robert L. Dabney, *Discussions* (1890; reprint, Harrisonburg, Vir.: Sprinkle Publications, 1992), 1:692–93.

APPENDIX A

Samuel Miller's Argument from Church History

THE FOLLOWING MATERIAL is an excerpt from pages 21–32 of Samuel Miller's book Infant Baptism Scriptural and Reasonable (Philadelphia: Presbyterian Board of Publication, 1834). Miller was a professor of ecclesiastical history and church government at Princeton Theological Seminary. The authoritative proof for the practice of infant baptism comes from Scripture alone, as already presented in this book. However, given the biblical truth of the practice, we would expect to find confirming evidence from church history. Miller provides this confirming evidence.

The history of the Christian Church from the apostolic age, furnishes an argument of irresistible force in favour of the divine authority of infant baptism.

I can assure you, my friends, with the utmost candour and confidence, after much careful inquiry on the subject, that, for more than fifteen hundred years after the birth of Christ, there was not a single society of professing Christians on earth, who opposed infant baptism on any thing like the grounds which distinguish our modern Baptist brethren. It is an *undoubted fact,* that the people known in ecclesiastical history under the name of the Anabaptists, who arose in Germany, in the year 1522, were the very first body of people, in the whole Christian world, who rejected the baptism of infants, on the principles now adopted by the Antipœdobaptist body. This, I am aware, will be regarded as an untenable position by some of the ardent friends of the Baptist cause; but nothing can be more certain than that it is even so. Of this a short induction of particulars will afford conclusive evidence.

Tertullian, about two hundred years after the birth of Christ, is the first man of whom we read in ecclesiastical history, as speaking a word against infant baptism; and he, while he recognises the existence and prevalence of the practice, and expressly recommends that infants be baptized, if they are not likely to survive the period of infancy; yet advises that, where there is a prospect of their living, baptism be delayed until a late period in life. But what was the reason of this advice? The moment we look at the reason, we see that it avails nothing to the cause in support of which it is sometimes produced. Tertullian adopted the superstitious idea, that baptism was accompanied with the remission of all past sins; and that sins committed after baptism were peculiarly dangerous. He, therefore, advised, that not merely infants, but young men and young women; and even young widows and widowers should postpone their baptism until the period of youthful appetite and passion should have passed. In short, he advised that, in all cases in which death was not likely to intervene, baptism should be postponed, until the subjects of it should have arrived at a period of life, when they would be no longer in danger of being led astray by youthful lusts. And thus, for more than a century after the age of Tertullian, we find some of the most conspicuous converts to the Christian faith, postponing baptism till the close of life. Constantine the Great, we are told, though a professing Christian for many years before, was not baptized till after the commencement of his last illness. The same fact is recorded of a number of other distinguished converts to Christianity, about and after that time. But, surely, advice and facts of this kind make nothing in favour of the system of our Baptist brethren. Indeed, taken altogether, their historical bearing is strongly in favour of our system.

The next persons that we hear of as calling in question the propriety of infant baptism, were the small body of people in France, about twelve hundred years after Christ, who followed a certain *Peter de Bruis,* and formed an inconsiderable section of the people known in ecclesiastical history under the general name of the *Waldenses.* This body maintained that infants ought not to be baptized, because they were incapable of salvation. They taught that none could be saved but those who wrought out their salvation by a long course of self-denial and labour. And as infants were incapable of thus "working out their own salvation," they held that making them the subjects of a sacramental seal, was an absurdity. But surely our Baptist brethren cannot be willing to consider these people as their predecessors, or to adopt their creed.

We hear no more of any society or organized body of *Antipœdobaptists,* until the sixteenth century, when they arose, as before stated, in Germany, and for the first time broached the doctrine of our modern Baptist brethren. As far as I have been able to discover, they were absolutely unknown in the whole Christian world, before that time.

But we have something more than mere negative testimony on this subject. It is not only certain, that we hear of no society of *Antipœdobaptists* resembling our present Baptist brethren, for more than fifteen hundred years after Christ; but we have positive and direct proof that, during the whole of that time, infant baptism was the general and unopposed practice of the Christian Church.

To say nothing of earlier intimations, wholly irreconcilable with any other practice than that of infant baptism, *Origen,* a Greek father of the third century, and decidedly the most learned man of his day, speaks in the most unequivocal terms of the baptism of infants, as the general practice of the church in his time, and as having been received from the Apostles. His testimony is as follows—"According to the usage of the church, baptism is given even to infants; when if there were nothing in infants which needed forgiveness and mercy, the grace of baptism would seem to be superfluous." (Homil. VII. in Levit. ch. 12.) Again; "Infants are baptized for the forgiveness of sins. Of what sins? Or, when have they sinned? Or, can there be any reason for the laver in their case, unless it be according to the sense which we have mentioned above, viz: that no one is free from pollution, though he has lived but one day upon earth? And because by baptism native pollution is taken away, therefore infants are baptized." (Homil. in Luc. 14.) Again: "For this cause it was that the church received an order from the Apostles to give baptism even to infants."[1]

The testimony of *Cyprian,* a Latin father of the third century, contemporary with *Origen,* is no less decisive. It is as follows:

In the year 253 after Christ, there was a Council of sixty-six bishops or pastors held at Carthage, in which Cyprian presided. To this Council, *Fidus,* a country pastor, presented the following question, which he wished them, by their united wisdom, to solve—viz. Whether it was necessary, in the administration of baptism, as of circumcision, to wait until the *eighth day;* or whether a child might be baptized at an earlier period after his birth? The question, it will be observed, was *not* whether infants ought to be baptized? *That* was taken for granted. But simply, whether it was necessary to wait until the *eighth day* after their birth? The Council came *unanimously* to the following decision, and transmitted it in a letter to the inquirer.

"Cyprian and the rest of the Bishops who were present in the Council, sixty-six in number, to Fidus, our brother, greeting:

"As to the case of Infants,—whereas you judge that they must not be baptized within two or three days after they are born, and that the rule of circumcision is to be observed, that no one should be baptized and sanctified before the eighth

day after he is born; we were all in the Council of a very different opinion. As for what you thought proper to be done, no
one was of your mind; but we all rather judged that the mercy
and grace of God is to be denied to no human being that is
born. This, therefore, dear brother, was our opinion in the
Council; that we ought not to hinder any person from baptism, and the grace of God, who is merciful and kind to us all.
And this rule, as it holds for all, we think more especially to be
observed in reference to infants, even to those newly born."
(Cyprian, Epist. 66.)

Surely no testimony can be more unexceptionable and
decisive than this. Lord Chancellor King, in his account of
the primitive church, after quoting what is given above, and
much more, subjoins the following remark—"Here, then is a
synodical decree for the baptism of infants, as formal as can
possibly be expected; which being the judgment of a synod,
is more authentic and cogent than that of a private father; it
being supposable that a private father might write his own
particular judgment and opinion only; but the determination of synod [and he might have added, the *unanimous* determination of a synod of sixty-six members] denotes the
common practice and usage of the whole church."[2]

The famous *Chrysostom*, a Greek father, who flourished
towards the close of the fourth century, having had occasion
to speak of circumcision, and of the inconvenience and pain
which attended its dispensation, proceeds to say—"But *our* circumcision, I mean the grace of *baptism*, gives cure without pain,
and procures to us a thousand benefits, and fills us with the
grace of the Spirit; and it has *no determinate time*, as that had;
but one that is in the *very beginning of his age*, or one that is in
the middle of it, or one that is in his old age, may receive this
circumcision made without hands; in which there is no trouble to be undergone but to throw off the load of sins, and to
receive pardon for all past offences." (Homil. 40. *in Genesin.*)

Passing by the testimony of several other conspicuous
writers of the third and fourth centuries, in support of the
fact, that infant baptism was generally practised when they

wrote, I shall detain you with only one testimony more in relation to the history of this ordinance. It is that of *August-ine,* one of the most pious, learned and venerable fathers of the Christian Church, who lived a little more than three hundred years after the Apostles,—taken in connexion with that of *Pelagius,* the learned heretic, who lived at the same time. Augustine had been pleading against Pelagius, in favour of the doctrine of original sin. In the course of this plea, he asks—"Why are infants baptized for the remission of sins, if they have no sin?" At the same time intimating to Pelagius, that if he would be consistent with himself, his denial of original sin must draw after it the denial of infant baptism. The reply of Pelagius is striking an unequivocal. "Baptism," says he, "ought to be administered to infants, with the same sacramental words which are used in the case of adult per-sons."—"Men slander me as if I denied the sacrament of baptism to infants."—"*I never heard of any, not even the most impious heretic, who denied baptism to infants;* for who can be so impious as to hinder infants from being baptized, and born again in Christ, and so make them miss the kingdom of God?" Again: Augustine remarks, in reference to Pelagians—"Since they grant that infants must be baptized, as not being able to *resist the authority of the whole church, which was doubtless delivered by our Lord and his Apostles;* they must consequently grant that they stand in need of the benefit of the Mediator; that being offered by the sacrament, and by the charity of the faithful, and so being incorporated into Christ's body, they may be reconciled to God," &c. Again, speaking of cer-tain heretics at Carthage, who, though they acknowledge infant baptism, took wrong views of its meaning, Augustine remarks—"They, *minding the Scriptures, and the authority of the whole church,* and the form of the sacrament itself, see well that baptism in infants is for the remission of sins." Further, in his work against the *Donatists,* the same writer speaking of baptized infants obtaining salvation without the personal ex-ercise of faith, he says—"which *the whole body of the church holds,* as delivered to them in the case of little infants baptized; who certainly cannot believe with the heart unto righteousness, or confess with the mouth unto salvation, nay, by their crying and noise while the sacrament is administering, they disturb the holy mysteries: and yet *no Christian man* will say that they are baptized to no purpose." Again, he says—"The custom of our mother the church in baptizing infants must not be disregarded, nor be accounted needless, nor believed to be anything else than *an ordinance delivered to us from the Apostles.*" In short, those who will be at the trouble to consult the large extracts from the writings of Augustine, among other Christian fathers, in the learned *Wall's* history of Infant Baptism, will find that venerable father declaring again and again that he never met with any Christian, either of the general church, or of any of the sects, nor with any writer, who owned the authority of Scripture, who taught any other doctrine than that infants were to be baptized for the remission of sin. Here, then, were two men, undoubtedly among the most learned then in the world—Augustine and Pelagius; the former as familiar probably with the writings of all the distinguished fathers who had gone before him, as any man of his time; the latter also a man of great learning and talents, who had travelled over the greater part of the Christian world; who both declare, about three hundred years after the apostolic age, that they never saw or heard of any one who called himself a Christian, not even the most impious heretic, no nor any writer who claimed to believe in the Scriptures, who denied the baptism of infants. (See Wall's History, Part I. ch. 15–19.) Can the most incredulous reader, who is not fast bound in the fetters of invincible prejudice, hesitate to admit, first, that these men verily believed that infant baptism had been the universal practice of the church from the days of the Apostles; and, secondly, that, situated and informed as they were, it was impossible that they should be mistaken?

The same Augustine, in his *Epistle to Boniface,* while he expresses an opinion that the parents are the proper persons to offer up their children to God in baptism, if they be good faithful Christians; yet thinks proper to mention that others may, with propriety, in special cases, perform the same kind office of Christian charity. He says: "You see," says he, "that a great many are offered, not by their parents, but by any other persons, as infant slaves are sometimes offered by their masters. And sometimes when the parents are dead, the infants are baptized, being offered by any that can afford to show this compassion on them. And sometimes infants whom their parents have cruelly exposed, may be taken up and offered in baptism by those who have no children, nor design to have any." Again, in his book against the *Donatists*, speaking directly of infant baptism, he says—"If any one ask for divine authority in this matter, although that which *the whole church practises*, which *was not instituted by councils*, but was *ever in use*, is very reasonably believed to be no other than a thing delivered by the authority of the Apostles; yet we may besides take a true estimate, how much the sacrament of baptism does avail infants, by the circumcision which God's ancient people received. For Abraham was justified before he received circumcision, as Cornelius was endued with the Holy Spirit before he was baptized. And yet the apostle says of Abraham, that he received the sign of circumcision, 'a seal of the righteousness of faith,' by which he had in heart believed, and it had been 'counted to him for righteousness.' Why then was he commanded to circumcise all his male infants on the eighth day, when they could not yet believe with the heart, that it might be counted to them for righteousness; but for this reason, because the sacrament is, in itself of great importance? Therefore, as in Abraham, 'the righteousness of faith' went before, and circumcision, 'the seal of the righteousness of faith' came after; so in Cornelius, the spiritual sanctification by the gift of the Holy Spirit went before, and the sacrament of regeneration, by the laver of baptism, came after. And as Isaac, who was circumcised the eighth day, the seal of the righteousness of faith went before, and (as he was a follower of his father's faith) the righteousness itself, the seal whereof had gone before in his infancy, came after; so in infants baptized, the sacrament of regeneration goes before,

baptized by the Romish priests, they deferred the perfor-
mance of it as long as possible, because they detested the
human inventions annexed to the institution of that holy
sacrament, which they looked upon as so many pollutions of
it. And by reason of their pastors, whom they called *Barbes,*
being often abroad travelling in the service of the church,
they could not have baptism administered to their children
by them. They, therefore, sometimes kept them long without
it. On account of which delay, the priests have charged them
with that reproach. To which charge not only their adversar-
ies have given credit, *but also many of those who have approved
of their lives and faith in all other respects.*"[3]

It being so plainly a fact, established by their own unequivocal and repeated testimony, that the great body of the
Waldenses were Pœdobaptists, on what ground is it that our
Baptist brethren assert, and that some have been found to
credit the assertion, that those venerable witnesses of the
truth rejected the baptism of infants? The answer is easy and
ample. A small section of the people bearing the general
name of Waldenses, followers of Peter de Bruis, who were
mentioned in a preceding page while they agreed with the
mass of their denomination in most other matters, differed
from them in regard to the subject of infant baptism. They
held, as before stated, that infants were not capable of salvation; that Christian salvation is of such a nature that none
can partake of it but those who undergo a course of rigorous
self-denial and labour in its pursuit. Those who die in infancy
not being capable of this, the Petrobrussians held that they
were not capable of salvation; and, this being the case, that
they ought not to be baptized. This, however, is not the
doctrine of our Baptists brethren; and, of course, furnishes
no support to their creed or practice. But the decisive answer is, that the Petrobrussians were a very small fraction of
the great Waldensian body; probably not more than a thirtieth or fortieth part of the whole. The great mass of the
denomination however, as such, declare, in their Confession
of Faith, and in various public documents, that they held,

and that their fathers before them, for many generations, always held, to infant baptism. The Petrobrussians, in this respect, forsook the doctrine and practice of their fathers, and departed from the proper and established Waldensian creed. If there be truth in the plainest records of ecclesiastical history, this is an undoubted fact. In short the real state of this case may be illustrated by the following representation. Suppose it were alleged that the Baptists in the United States are in the habit of keeping the seventh day of the week as their Sabbath? Would the statement be true? By no means. There is, indeed, a small section of the Antipœdobaptist body in the United States, usually styled "Seventh day Baptists"—probably not a thirtieth part of the whole body—who observe Saturday in each week as their Sabbath. But, notwithstanding this, the proper representation, no doubt is,—(the only representation that a faithful historian of facts would pronounce correct)—that the Baptists in this country, as a general body, observe "the Lord's day" as their Sabbath. You may rest assured, my friends, that this statement most exactly illustrates the real fact with regard to the Waldenses as Pœdobaptists. Twenty-nine parts, at least, out of thirty, of the whole of that body of witnesses for the truth, were undoubtedly Pœdobaptists. The remaining thirtieth part departed from the faith of their fathers in regard to baptism, but departed on principles altogether unlike those of our modern Baptist brethren.

I have only one fact more to state in reference to the pious Waldenses, and that is, that soon after the opening of the Reformation by Luther, they sought intercourse with the Reformed churches of Geneva and France; held communion with them; received ministers from them; and appeared eager to testify their respect and affection for them as "brethren in the Lord." Now it is well known that the churches of Geneva and France, at this time, were in the habitual use of *infant* baptism. This single fact is sufficient to prove that the Waldenses were Pœdobaptists. If they had adopted the doctrine of our Baptist brethren, and laid the same stress on it with them, it is mani-

fest that such intercourse would have been wholly out of the
question.

If these historical statements be correct, and that they are
so, is just as well attested as any facts whatever in the annals of
the church, the amount of the whole is conclusive, is *demon-
strative*, that, for fifteen hundred years after Christ, the practice of infant baptism was universal; that to this general fact
there was absolutely no exception, in the whole Christian
church, which, on principle, or even analogy, can countenance
in the least degree, modern Anti-pœdobaptism; that from the
time of the Apostles to the time of Luther, the general, unopposed, established practice of the church was to regard the
infant seed of believers as members of the church, and, as such,
to baptize them.

But this is not all. If the doctrine of our Baptist brethren
be correct; that is, if infant baptism be a corruption and a nul-
lity; then it follows, from the foregoing historical statements,
most inevitably, that the ordinance of baptism was lost for fifteen hundred years: yes, entirely lost, from the apostolic age
till the sixteenth century. For there was manifestly, "no society, during that long period, of fifteen centuries, but what was
in the habit of baptizing infants." *God had no church, then, in the
world for so long a period!* Can this be admitted? Surely not by
any one who believes in the perpetuity and indestructibility of
the household of faith.

Nay, if the principle of our Baptist brethren be correct,
the ordinance of baptism is irrecoverably lost altogether; that
is, irrevocably without a miracle. Because if, during the long
tract of time that has been mentioned, there was no true baptism in the church; and if none but baptized persons were capable of administering true baptism to others? the consequence
is plain; there is no true baptism now in the world! But can
this be believed? Can we imagine that the great Head of the
Church would permit one of his own precious ordinances to
be banished entirely from the church for many centuries, much
less to be totally lost? Surely the thought is abhorrent to every
Christian feeling.

NOTES

1. Comment. in Epist. ad Romanos. Lib. 5.
2. Inquiry into the Constitution, &c. Part II. Chap. 3.
3. See John Paul Perrin's account of the Doctrine and Order of the Waldenses and Albigenses; Sir Samuel Morland's do.; and also Leger's Histoire Generale des Eglises Vaudoises. Mr. William Jones, a Baptist, in a work entitled, a History of the Waldenses, in two volumes octavo, professes to give a full account of the Faith and Order of these pious witnesses of the truth; but, so far as I have observed, carefully leaves out of all their public formularies and other documents, every thing which would disclose their Pœdobaptist principles and practise! On this artifice comment is unnecessary.

Appendix B

The Similarities of Circumcision and Baptism

The table below shows the many ways in which circumcision and baptism are alike. Although there was a change in outward form, there was no change in meaning when baptism replaced circumcision as the sign and seal of the covenant of grace.

CIRCUMCISION AND BAPTISM:	REFERENCES:
Are initiatory rites	Gen. 17:10–11; Matt. 28:19; Acts 2:38–39; 8:12–13
Signify an inward reality	Rom. 2:28–29; Col. 2:11–12; Phil. 3:3
Picture the death of the old man of sin	Rom. 6:3–7; Col. 2:11–12
Represent repentance	Jer. 4:4; 9:25; Lev. 26:40–41; Acts 2:38
Represent regeneration	Rom. 2:28–29; Titus 3:5
Represent justification by faith	Rom. 4:11–12; Col. 2:11–14
Represent a cleansed heart	Deut. 10:16; 30:6; Isa. 52:1; Acts 22:16; Titus 3:5–7
Represent union and communion with God	Gen. 17:7; Ex. 19:5–6; Deut. 7:6; Heb. 8:10
Indicate citizenship in Israel	Gen. 17:4; Gal. 3:26–29; Eph. 2:12–13; 4:5
Indicate separation from the world	Ex. 12:48; 2 Cor. 6:14–18; Eph. 2:12
Can lead to either blessings or curses	Rom. 2:25; 1 Cor. 10:1–12; 11:28–30

Index of Scripture

Robert R. (Randy) Booth received a Bachelor of Science degree in history from East Texas State University and has completed graduate studies in Christian apologetics. Formerly a Baptist pastor for ten years, he now is pastor of Grace Covenant Presbyterian Church, Nacogdoches, Texas. He is also the director of Covenant Media Foundation and serves on the faculty of the Dabney Theological Study Center in Monroe, Louisiana. He and his wife, Marinell, have three grown children.